Beginner

Student's Book

New Headway

English Course

Liz and John Soars

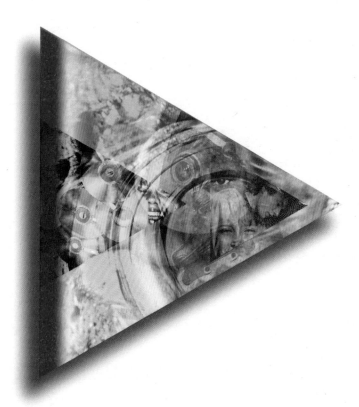

OXFORD
UNIVERSITY PRESS

CONTENTS

3

1 Hello!

am/are/is · my/your · This is . . . · How are you? · What's this in English? · Numbers 1–10 · Plurals

T 1.1 Say your name.

Hello. I'm Lisa.

Hello. I'm Marek.

WHAT'S YOUR NAME?

am / are / is, my / your

1 **T 1.2** Read and listen.

Sandra Hello. I'm Sandra. What's your name?
Hiro My name's Hiro.
Sandra Hello, Hiro.

T 1.2 Listen and repeat.

GRAMMAR SPOT

I'**m** = I am
name'**s** = name is
What'**s** = What is

2 Stand up and practise.

Hello. I'm _____ .
What's your name?

My name's _____ .

This is . . .

3 **T 1.3** Read and listen.

Sandra John, this is Hiro Shiga. Hiro, this is John Mason.
Hiro Hello, John.
John Hello, Hiro.

T 1.3 Listen and repeat.

4 Practise in groups of three.

_____, *this is* _____.
_____, *this is* _____.

Hello, _____.

Hello, _____.

How are you?

5 **T 1.4** Read and listen.

T 1.4 Listen and repeat.

6 **T 1.5** Read and listen.

T 1.5 Listen and repeat.

7 Answer your teacher.

8 Stand up and practise.

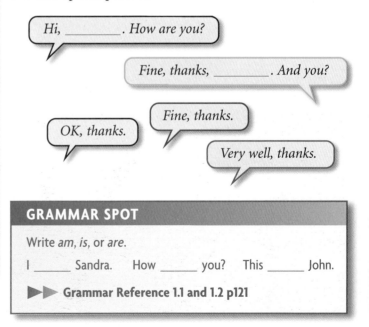

GRAMMAR SPOT

Write *am*, *is*, or *are*.

I _____ Sandra.   How _____ you?   This _____ John.

▶▶ **Grammar Reference 1.1 and 1.2 p121**

PRACTICE

Introductions

1 Complete the conversations.

1 **A** Hello. <u>My</u> name's Anna.
   <u>What's</u> your name?
   B Ben.

2 **C** Hello. My _____ Carla.
   What's _____ name?
   D _____ name's David.

T 1.6 Listen and check. Practise the conversations.

2 Complete the conversations.

1 **B** _____, Anna. _____ are you?
   A Fine, thanks, Ben. _____ _____?
   B _____ well, thanks.

2 **D** Hi, Carla. _____ _____ you?
   C _____, thanks. _____ _____?
   D OK, _____.

T 1.7 Listen and check. Practise the conversations.

3 **T 1.8** Listen and number the lines in the conversation.

- ☐ Fine, thanks.
- ☐ I'm OK, thanks. And you?
- ☐ 1 Hello. My name's Rita. What's your name?
- ☐ Hello, Tina. Hello, Mary.
- ☐ I'm Tina, and this is Mary.
- ☐ Hello, Rita. How are you?

T 1.8 Listen, check, and practise.

▶▶ **Grammar Reference 1.3 p121**

VOCABULARY

What's this in English?

1 Write the words.

a book	a camera	a car
a photograph	a computer	a bag
a hamburger	a television	
a sandwich	a house	

1 a photograph

2

3

4

5

6

7

8

9

10

2 **T 1.9** Listen and repeat the words.

3 **T 1.10** Listen and repeat.

> *What's this in English?*

> *It's a photograph.*

Work with a partner. Point to a picture. Ask and answer questions.

4 Go to things in the room. Ask your teacher.

> *What's this in English?*

EVERYDAY ENGLISH

Numbers 1–10 and plurals

1 **T 1.11** Read and listen. Practise the numbers.

1 one   **2** two   **4** four   **5** five   **7** seven   **8** eight   **9** nine   **10** ten
3 three   **6** six

Say the numbers round the class.

2 Write the numbers.

1 ten | sandwiches

2 | books

3 | bags

4 | computers

5 | houses

6 | hamburgers

7 | cameras

8 | photographs

9 | cars

10 | students

T 1.12 Listen and check.

3 **T 1.13** Listen and repeat.

/s/	/z/	/ɪz/
books	cars	sandwiches
photographs	computers	houses
students	hamburgers	
	cameras	
	televisions	
	bags	

> **GRAMMAR SPOT**
>
> | Singular | Plural |
> |---|---|
> | one book | two books |
> | one sandwich | ten sandwiches |
>
> ▶▶ **Grammar Reference 1.4 p121**

2 Your world

STARTER

1 Find the countries on the map on p13. Find your country on the map.

Australia Brazil England France Italy Japan Spain the United States

2 **T 2.1** Listen and repeat.

WHERE ARE YOU FROM?

he/she, his/her

1 **T 2.2** Read and listen.

Hiro	Where are you from, Sandra?
Sandra	I'm from Spain. Where are you from?
Hiro	I'm from Japan. From Tokyo.

T 2.2 Listen and repeat.

2 Where are you from? Stand up and practise.

3 **T 2.3** Read, listen, and repeat.

His name's Hiro. He's from Japan.

Her name's Sandra. She's from Spain.

GRAMMAR SPOT

he**'s** = he is   she**'s** = she is

▶▶ **Grammar Reference 2.1 and 2.2 p121**

4 Complete the sentences.

1 His name's Rick.
He's from the United States.

2 ____ name's Sonia.
She's ____
____.

3 ____ name's Jack.
He's ____
____.

4 ____ name's Sergio.
He's ____
____.

5 ____ name's Marie.
She's ____
____.

6 ____ name's Kim.
She's ____
____.

T 2.4 Listen and check. Repeat the sentences.

Questions

5 **T 2.5** Listen and repeat the questions.

What's his name?   Where's he from?
What's her name?   Where's she from?

6 Ask and answer questions about the people in the photographs.

What's her name?

Her name's Sandra.

Where's she from?

She's from Spain.

> **GRAMMAR SPOT**
>
> **1** Where**'s** = Where is
> **2** Complete the questions with *is* or *are*.
>   Where _____ she from?
>   Where _____ he from?
>   Where _____ you from?
> ►► **Grammar Reference 2.3 p121**

PRACTICE

Cities and countries

1 Where are the cities? Ask and answer.

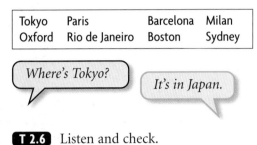

| Tokyo | Paris | Barcelona | Milan |
| Oxford | Rio de Janeiro | Boston | Sydney |

Where's Tokyo?

It's in Japan.

T 2.6 Listen and check.

2 Work with a partner.
Student A Look at the photos on this page.
Student B Look at the photos on p138.

Ask questions and write the answers.

What's her name?

Where's she from?

Talking about you

3 Ask about the students in the class.

What's her name?

Her name's Chantal.

Where's she from?

She's from France. From Paris.

What's his name?

His name's Luc.

Where's he from?

He's from Paris, too.

1

Her name's Mayumi.
She's from Tokyo.

2

Her name's Carol.
She's from Oxford.

4

6

7

His name's Ted.
He's from Boston.

His name's Pierre.
He's from Paris.

His name's Adam.
He's from Sydney.

Questions and answers

4 **T 2.7** Listen and complete the conversation. Practise it.

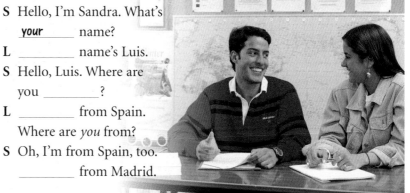

S Hello, I'm Sandra. What's ___your___ name?
L _____ name's Luis.
S Hello, Luis. Where are you _____?
L _____ from Spain.
Where are *you* from?
S Oh, I'm from Spain, too. _____ from Madrid.

5 **T 2.8** Listen and write the countries.

1 Gérard: **France**
Akemi: _____

2 Charles: _____
Bud: _____

3 Loretta and Jason:
_____

6 Match the questions and answers.

1 Where are you from?	His name's Luis.
2 What's her name?	He's from Madrid.
3 What's his name?	It's in Canada.
4 Where's he from?	I'm from Brazil.
5 What's this in English?	Fine, thanks.
6 How are you?	Her name's Irena.
7 Where's Toronto?	It's a computer.

T 2.9 Listen and check.

Check it

7 Tick (✓) the correct sentence.

1 ☐ My name Sandra.
✓ My name's Sandra.

2 ☐ What's he's name?
☐ What's his name?

3 ☐ 'What's his name?' 'Luis.'
☐ 'What's her name?' 'Luis.'

4 ☐ He's from Spain.
☐ His from Spain.

5 ☐ Where she from?
☐ Where's she from?

6 ☐ What's her name?
☐ What's she name?

READING AND LISTENING
Where are they from?

1 **T 2.10** Read and listen.

This is a photograph of Miguel and Glenna da Costa from Rio de Janeiro. They are in New York. Miguel is from Brazil, and Glenna is from Toronto in Canada. They are married. Glenna is a doctor. Her hospital is in the centre of Rio. Miguel is a teacher. His school is in the centre of Rio, too.

2 Complete the sentences.

1 Miguel is from _____.
2 He's a _____.
3 His school is in the _____ of Rio.
4 Glenna is from _____ in Canada.
5 She's a _____.
6 Her _____ is in the centre of Rio.
7 They _____ in New York.
8 They are _____.

GRAMMAR SPOT

Write *is* or *are*.
She _____ a doctor.
He _____ a teacher.
They _____ from Brazil.

▶▶ **Grammar Reference 2.4 p121**

3 Write questions with *what* and *where* about Miguel and Glenna. Ask a partner.

What/name? Where/from? Where/school? Where/hospital?

What's his name?

Where are they?

EVERYDAY ENGLISH
Numbers 11–30

1 Say the numbers 1–10 round the class.

2 [T 2.11] Listen, read, and repeat.

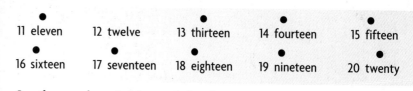

| • 11 eleven | • 12 twelve | • 13 thirteen | • 14 fourteen | • 15 fifteen |
| • 16 sixteen | • 17 seventeen | • 18 eighteen | • 19 nineteen | • 20 twenty |

Say the numbers 1–20 round the class.

3 Write the numbers your teacher says. Say the numbers your teacher writes.

4 Match the numbers.

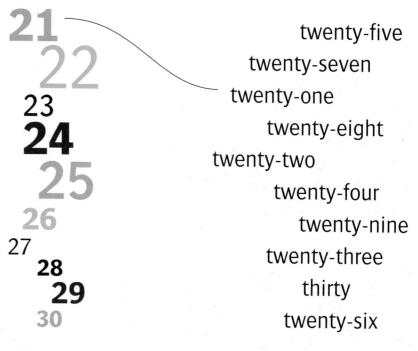

21   twenty-five
22   twenty-seven
23   twenty-one
24   twenty-eight
25   twenty-two
26   twenty-four
27   twenty-nine
28   twenty-three
29   thirty
30   twenty-six

[T 2.12] Listen and repeat. Say the numbers 1–30 round the class.

5 [T 2.13] Listen and tick (✓) the numbers you hear.

1 **22**	12 ✓	10	20
2 17	15	**16**	14
3 21	**29**	19	**9**
4 **11**	**7**	**17**	27
5 23	3	13	30

6 Work with a partner.

Student A Write five numbers. Say them to your partner.
Student B Write the numbers you hear. **14 24 …**

3 Personal information

Jobs • am/are/is – negatives and questions • Address, phone number • Social expressions

STARTER

1 Match the jobs and the pictures.

> a police officer   a nurse   a student   ~~a teacher~~   a shop assistant   a taxi driver   a businessman   a doctor

1 a teacher	**2**	**3**	**4**
5	**6**	**7**	**8**

T 3.1 Listen and repeat.

2 What's your job? Ask and answer.

What's your job?

I'm a student.

I'm a businessman.

WHAT'S HER JOB?
Negatives – *isn't*

1 **T 3.2** Listen and repeat.

What's his job? He's a teacher.
What's her job? She's a doctor.

Look at the pictures. Ask and answer questions with a partner.

2 **T 3.3** Listen and repeat.

He isn't a student. He's a teacher.
She isn't a nurse. She's a doctor.

Make more negative and positive sentences.

GRAMMAR SPOT

She **isn't** a nurse.	*isn't* = is not	This is negative.
He**'s a** teacher.	*'s* = is	This is positive.

He/She isn't a _____ .

He/She's a _____ .

18   Unit 3 · Personal information

Questions and short answers

3 Read the information.

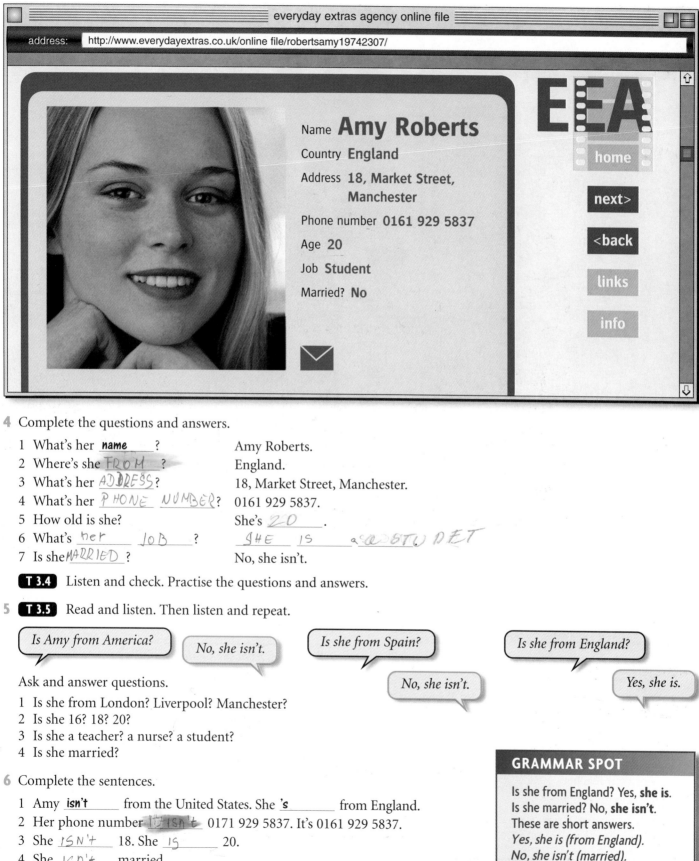

everyday extras agency online file

address: http://www.everydayextras.co.uk/online file/robertsamy19742307/

Name **Amy Roberts**

Country **England**

Address **18, Market Street, Manchester**

Phone number **0161 929 5837**

Age **20**

Job **Student**

Married? **No**

home
next>
<back
links
info

4 Complete the questions and answers.

1 What's her **name**   ?   Amy Roberts.
2 Where's she FROM   ?   England.
3 What's her ADDRESS?   18, Market Street, Manchester.
4 What's her P HONE NUMBER? 0161 929 5837.
5 How old is she?   She's 20   .
6 What's her   JOB   ?   SHE IS   a STUDET
7 Is she MARRIED ?   No, she isn't.

T 3.4 Listen and check. Practise the questions and answers.

5 **T 3.5** Read and listen. Then listen and repeat.

Is Amy from America?   *No, she isn't.*   *Is she from Spain?*   *Is she from England?*

No, she isn't.   *Yes, she is.*

Ask and answer questions.

1 Is she from London? Liverpool? Manchester?
2 Is she 16? 18? 20?
3 Is she a teacher? a nurse? a student?
4 Is she married?

6 Complete the sentences.

1 Amy **isn't**   from the United States. She **'s**   from England.
2 Her phone number isn't 0171 929 5837. It's 0161 929 5837.
3 She ISN't 18. She IS   20.
4 She isn't   married.

> **GRAMMAR SPOT**
>
> Is she from England? Yes, **she is.**
> Is she married? No, **she isn't.**
> These are short answers.
> *Yes, she is (from England).*
> *No, she isn't (married).*

WHAT'S YOUR JOB?
Negatives and short answers

1 **T 3.6** Listen and complete the conversation.

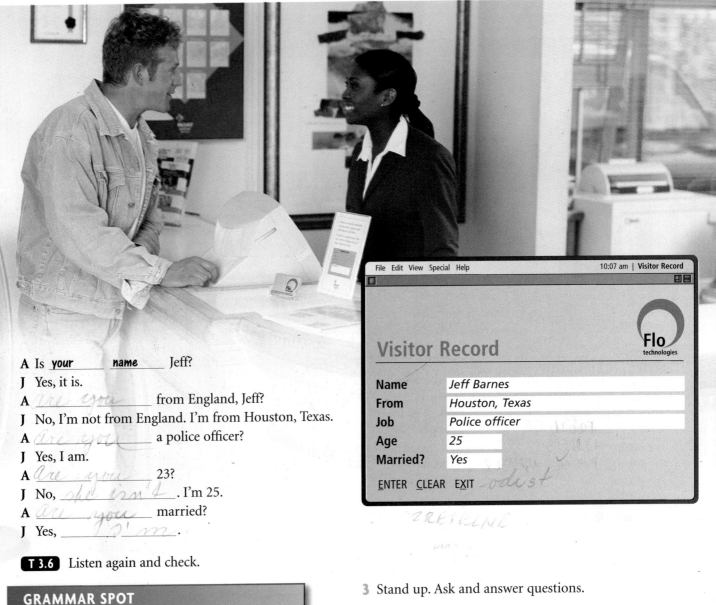

A Is **your   name** Jeff?

J Yes, it is.

A *are you* from England, Jeff?

J No, I'm not from England. I'm from Houston, Texas.

A *are you* a police officer?

J Yes, I am.

A *are you* 23?

J No, *she isn't*. I'm 25.

A *are you* married?

J Yes, *I'm*.

T 3.6 Listen again and check.

> File Edit View Special Help   10:07 am | Visitor Record
>
> ## Visitor Record   Flo
>   technologies
>
> **Name**   Jeff Barnes
> **From**   Houston, Texas
> **Job**   Police officer
> **Age**   25
> **Married?** Yes
>
> ENTER CLEAR EXIT

GRAMMAR SPOT

1 **I'm not** from England. *I'm not* = I am not
  This is negative.

2 Yes, **I am**. No, **I'm not**.   Yes, **it is**. No, **it isn't**.
  These are short answers.

▶▶ **Grammar Reference 3.1 p122**

2 Answer your teacher.

Are you from Italy?

Yes, I am.

No, I'm not.

3 Stand up. Ask and answer questions.

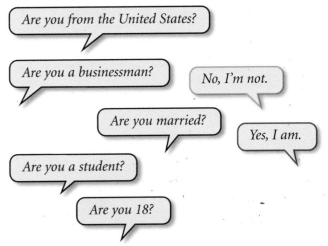

Are you from the United States?

Are you a businessman?

No, I'm not.

Are you married?

Yes, I am.

Are you a student?

Are you 18?

PRACTICE

Listening and speaking

1 **T 3.7** Listen to the conversations. Complete the chart.

Name	Giovanni Tomba	Diana Black
Country	Italy	United States ~~new york~~ NEW YORK
City/Town	ROME ITALY	new york
Phone number	069 448 13 9	212 463 9145
Age	23	29
Job	TAXI DRIVER	Shop assistant
Married?	No	Yes

Diana

Giovanni

T 3.7 Listen again and check.

2 Ask and answer the questions with a partner. Use short answers.

Is Giovanni from Milan? Is Diana from the United States?
Is he a nurse? Is she a teacher?
Is his phone number 06 944 8139? Is she twenty-nine?

Talking about you

3 Complete the questions.

1 __What's__   __your__   name?
2 _____ _____ you from?
3 _____ _____ phone number?
4 How old _____ _____ ?
5 _____ _____ job?
6 _____ _____ married?

In groups, ask and answer the same questions.

4 Write about one student.

Her name's Marie-Ange. She's from France. Her phone number is ...

Check it   HOMEWORK!!!

5 Tick (✓) the correct sentence.

1 ☐ She's name's Janelle.
   ☑ Her name's Janelle.
2 ☐ Her job is teacher.
   ☑ She's a teacher.
3 ☑ Are you from Spain?
   ☐ Is you from Spain?
4 ☐ He's phone number is 796542.
   ☑ His phone number is 796542.
5 ☑ How old is she?
   ☐ How old she is?
6 ☐ She is no married.
   ☑ She isn't married.
7 ☐ Are you married?   Yes, I'm.
   ☑ Are you married?   Yes, I am.

READING AND SPEAKING

A pop group

1 Read about the pop group *4 x 4*.

Melanie   Yves   Cath   George

This is the pop group **4x4** (Four by Four). Melanie Ryan is from Australia. Yves Lacoste is from France. Cath and George Walters are from England. They're on tour in the United States. '

'We're in New York. We're at the Radio City Music Hall. It's great!'
Who is married in *4x4*? Yves: '**I'm not married.**' George and Cath: '**We aren't married!**' Melanie: '**I am!**'

2 Complete the sentences.

1 The name of the group _____.
2 They _____ _____ from Australia.
3 Cath and George Walters _____ _____ England.
4 _____ _____ _____ France.
5 'We _____ on tour in the United States.'

3 **T 3.8** Listen and answer the questions.

1 How old is Melanie?
2 How old are Cath and George?
3 How old is Yves?
4 Who's married? Who isn't married?

GRAMMAR SPOT

We**'re** in New York.	*we're* = we are
We **aren't** married. This is negative.	*we aren't* = we are not

▶▶ **Grammar Reference 3.2 p122**

---

4 Work in groups of four. You are a pop group.

- What are your names?
- What's the name of the group?
- How old are you?
- Where are you now?
- Where are you from?

Ask and answer questions with another group.

EVERYDAY ENGLISH
Social expressions

1 Complete the conversations. Use these words.

| Good afternoon   Good night   Good evening   Good morning   Goodbye |

1
A _Good morning_.
B _GOOD MORNING_, Mr Brown.

2
A _GOOD AFTERNOON_. The Grand Hotel.
B _-//- -//-_.

3
A _GOOD EVENING_, madam.
B _-//- -//-_.

4
A _GOOD NIGHT_.
B _-//- -//-_, Peter. Sleep well.

5
A _GOODBYE_.
B _-//-_. Have a good journey!

T 3.9 Listen and check. Practise the conversations.

2 **T 3.10** Listen and complete the conversations. Use these words.

| pardon   don't understand   don't know   sorry   thank you |

1 A What's this in English?
  B I _DON'T KNOW_.
  A It's a dictionary.

2 C *Hogy hívnak?*
  M I _DON'T UNDERSTAND_.
  C What's your name?
  M My name's Manuel. I'm from Spain.

3 A The homework is on page … of the Workbook.
  B _PARDON?_
  A The homework is on page *thirty* of the Workbook.
  B _____ _____.

3 Practise the conversations.

4 Family and friends

STARTER

1 Complete the table.

Subject pronoun	I	you	he	she	we	they
Possessive adjective	my	*your*	*his*	*her*	our	their

T 4.1 Listen and check.

2 Talk about things in the classroom.

> This is my book.

> This is our class.

> This is her bag.

SALLY'S FAMILY

Possessive 's – family relations

1 **T 4.2** Read and listen.

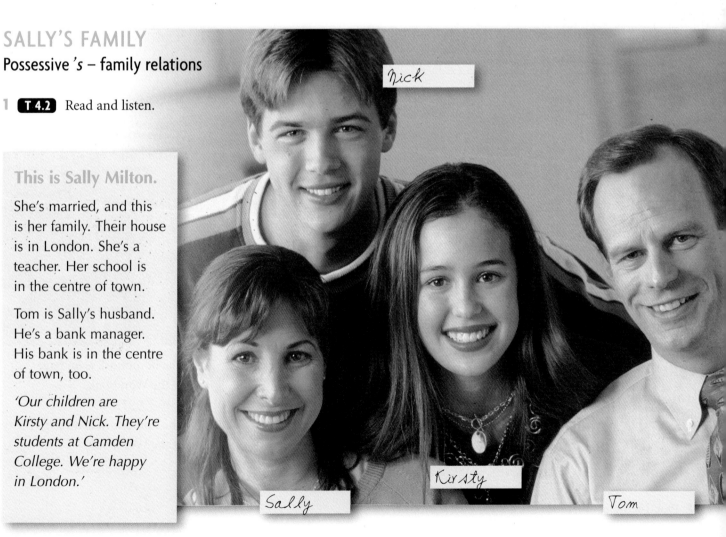

Nick

Kirsty

Sally

Tom

This is Sally Milton.

She's married, and this is her family. Their house is in London. She's a teacher. Her school is in the centre of town.

Tom is Sally's husband. He's a bank manager. His bank is in the centre of town, too.

'Our children are Kirsty and Nick. They're students at Camden College. We're happy in London.'

GRAMMAR SPOT

1 She**'s** married.   She**'s** a teacher.   *'s* = is

2 This is her family.
This is **Sally's** family.   *'s* = the family of Sally

3

his Tom's	bank	her Kirsty's	school

▶▶ **Grammar Reference 4.1–4.3 p123**

This is our house

Kirsty and Nick's college

2 Answer the questions.

1 Is Sally married?   **Yes, she is.**
2 Where's their house?   _____ 'ONDON
3 What is Sally's job?   SHE'S _____
4 Where's her school?   _____
5 What is Tom's job?   occupation, zamestnanie
6 Where is his bank?   _____
7 Are their children doctors?   NO THEY AREN'T
   THEY ARE STUDENTS

T 4.3 Listen and check.

3 **T 4.4** Listen and repeat.

♀	mother	daughter	sister	wife
♂	father	son	brother	husband

Plural	parents	children

4 **T 4.5** Look at the family tree. Listen and complete the sentences.

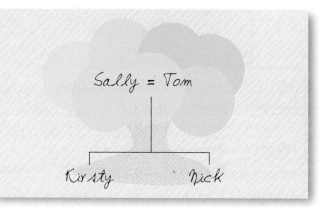

Sally = Tom

Kirsty   Nick

1 Sally is Tom's **wife**.
2 Tom is Sally's *husband*.
3 Kirsty is Sally and Tom's *child* DAUGHTR.
4 Nick is their *SON*.
5 Sally is Nick's *DAUGHTER*.
6 Tom is Kirsty's *daughter*.
7 Kirsty is Nick's *SISTER*.
8 Nick is Kirsty's *BROTHER*.
9 Sally and Tom are Kirsty and Nick's *PARENTS*.
10 Kirsty and Nick are Tom and Sally's *CHILDREN*.

T 4.5 Listen again and check.

5 Ask and answer questions.

Who's Nick?

He's Tom's son.

He's Kirsty's brother.

PRACTICE

The family

1 **T 4.6** Listen to Rachel Chang. Complete the information about her family.

	Name	Age	Job
Rachel's brother	STEVE	19	STUDENT
Rachel's mother	ROBIE	38	BUSINESSWOMAN
Rachel's father	BOB	44	

Bob?   **Grace?**   **Steve?**

2 Complete the sentences.

1 Steve is **Rachel's** brother.
2 Her _____ name is Grace.
3 Grace is Bob's _____.
4 'What's _____ job?' 'He's a businessman.'
5 'Where's _____ house?' 'It's in San Diego.'

3 Write the names of your family. Ask and answer questions with a partner.

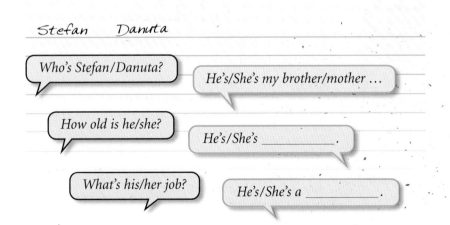

Stefan   Danuta

Who's Stefan/Danuta?

He's/She's my brother/mother …

How old is he/she?

He's/She's _____.

What's his/her job?

He's/She's a _____.

my/our/your . . .

4 Complete the sentences with a possessive adjective.

1 'What's **your** name?'
  'My name's Sally.'
2 'What are _their_ names?'
  'Our names are Kirsty and Nick.'
3 Jean-Paul and André are students.
  THEIR school is in Paris.
4 'My sister's married.'
  'What's _HER_ husband's name?'
5 'My brother's office is in New York.'
  'What's _HIS_ job?'
6 We are in _OUR_ English class.
7 'Mum and Dad are in Rome.'
  'What's _THEIR_ phone number?'

SALLY'S BROTHER
has/have

1 [T 4.7] Read and listen to David.

This is David Arnot and his family.

'We're from Wales. I have a small farm. My wife's name is Megan, and she has a job in town. She's a shop assistant. We have one child, Ben, and two dogs, Dylan and Dolly. My sister, Sally, and her husband, Tom, have a big house in London. They have two children. Tom has a very good job.'

2 Are the sentences true (✔) or false (✗)?

1. ☑ David's farm is in Wales.
2. ☑ David is Sally's brother.
3. ☒ His wife has a job in a hospital.
4. ☒ David and Megan have two children.
5. ☑ Their farm is big.
6. ☑ They have two dogs, Ben and Dolly.

3 [T 4.8] Listen and write the sentences. Practise them.

1. <u>I have a small farm in Wales.</u>
2. _____
3. _____
4. _____
5. _____
6. _____
7. _____

4 Write sentences about your family. Tell the class.

> GRAMMAR SPOT
>
> Complete the forms of the verb *have*.
>
> I _____
> You _____ have
> He _____ has
> She _____
> We _____
> They _____
>
> ▶▶ Grammar Reference 4.4 p123

We have a house in the country.

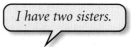
I have two sisters.

PRACTICE

has/have

1 Complete the sentences. Use *has* or *have*.

1 I **have** two brothers and a sister.
2 My parents *have* a house in the country.
3 My wife *has* a Japanese car.
4 My sister and I *have* a dog.
5 You *have* a very nice family.
6 Our school *has* fifteen classrooms.
7 We *have* English classes in the evening.

2 Talk about your school.

> *Our school is small.*

> *It has six classrooms.*

> *We have ten students in our class.*

Questions and answers

3 Match the questions and answers.

1 How is your mother?	Yes, we are.
2 What's your sister's job?	She's David's sister.
3 How old are your brothers?	It's in the centre of town.
4 Who is Sally?	She's very well, thank you.
5 Where is your office?	They're ten and thirteen.
6 Are you and your husband from Italy?	She's a nurse.

T 4.9 Listen and check.

Check it

4 Tick (✓) the correct sentence.

1 ☑ Mary's children are married.
  ☐ Mary is children are married.
2 ☐ What's your daughter name?
  ☑ What's your daughter's name?
3 ☐ What's he's job?
  ☑ What's his job?
4 ☑ They're from Germany.
  ☐ Their from Germany.
5 ☐ They're parents have a house in Bonn.
  ☑ Their parents have a house in Bonn.
6 ☐ My brother have a good job.
  ☑ My brother has a good job.
7 ☐ We house is in the centre of town.
  ☑ Our house is in the centre of town.

READING AND WRITING

My best friend

1 Read about Andy. Check the new words in your dictionary.

2 Match the photographs with a part of the text. Who are the people in the pictures?

My friend Andy

a My **best friend**'s name is Andy. He's **very nice**, and he's **really funny**. He's 22, and he's a student at **university**. He isn't married, **but** he has a **beautiful girlfriend**. Her name is Carrie, and she's American.

b Andy's parents have a **flat** in Manchester. It's **near** the centre of town. His father's a taxi driver, and his mother has a **part-time** job in a hospital.

c He has two sisters. Their names are Alison and Molly. They're **both** at school.

d Andy has **a lot of CDs**. His **favourite music** is rock 'n' roll, and his favourite **pop group** is *Mood*. He is **also** a **fan** of Manchester United!

When we're **together**, we **have a good time**.

1 a

3 <u>Underline</u> the correct information.

1 Andy is ...   <u>a student</u> / a bus driver / <u>nice</u> / American / <u>funny</u> / beautiful.

2 Andy has ...   <u>two sisters</u> / two brothers / a wife / <u>a girlfriend</u> / <u>a lot of CDs.</u>

3 Carrie is ...   Andy's sister / <u>Andy's girlfriend</u> / <u>American</u> / <u>beautiful.</u>

4 Andy's parents have ... <u>a house</u> / a flat / one daughter / <u>three children.</u>

5 Andy is ...   in a pop group called *Mood* / <u>a fan of *Mood*</u> / <u>a fan of Manchester United.</u>

4 Work with a partner. Talk about Andy.

> *Andy's a student. He's very ...*

5 Write about a good friend.

- My friend's name is ...
- She's / He's ...
- She / He has ...
- Her / His parents ...
- Her / His favourite ...

Write about family, job, music, sport ...

EVERYDAY ENGLISH
The alphabet

1 **T 4.10** Listen to the letters of the alphabet. Practise them.

A B C D E F G H I J K L M N O P Q R S T U V W X Y Z

2 Practise the letters in groups.

/eɪ/	a h j k		/əʊ/	o
/i:/	b c d e g p t v		/u:/	q u w
/e/	f l m n s x z		/ɑ:/	r
/aɪ/	i y			

3 **T 4.11** Listen to people spell their first name (Sally) and their surname (Milton). Write the names.

SALLY	MILTON
_____	_____
_____	_____
_____	_____
_____	_____

4 Practise spelling your name with a partner.

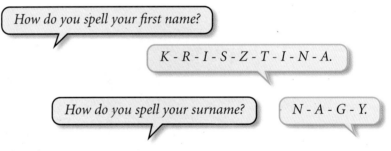

How do you spell your first name?

K - R - I - S - Z - T - I - N - A.

How do you spell your surname?   N - A - G - Y.

5 In pairs, ask and answer *How do you spell … ?* with words from the text about Andy on p28.

How do you spell 'friend'?   F - R - I - E - N - D.

6 Put the letters in the correct order. What's the country?

N E F A C R	**FRANCE**
N A P I S	SPAIN
L A R Z I B	BRAZIL
N A P A J	JAPAN
L A S A R U T A I	AUSTRALIA
Y L I A T	ITALIA
G A N E L D N	ENGLAND

On the phone

7 **T 4.12** Listen to the phone conversations.

1 **A** Good morning. The Grand Hotel.
   J Hello. The manager, please.
   A Certainly. And your name is?
   J José Gonzalez.
   A How do you spell your surname?
   J G – O – N – Z – A – L – E – Z.
   A Thank you.
   S Hello. Sam Jackson.
   J Mr Jackson, hello. This is José Gonzalez …

2 **B** Good afternoon. The Edinburgh English School.
   M Hello. The director, Annie Benton, please.
   B And your name is?
   M Mayumi Morioka.
   B M – A …
   M M – A – Y – U – M – I   M – O – R – I – O – K – A.
   B Thank you. … I'm sorry. She isn't in her office. What's your phone number?
   M It's Japan 3 5414 6443.
   B Thank you for telephoning. Goodbye.
   M Goodbye.

soac

Carrer Arcs 5, 12 ena planta, 08023 Barcelona
tel 93-306 785 04 fax 93-412 234 95

Señor José Gonzalez
export manager

tohoku *design*

2-21-10 #204 Akasaka Building
Sendagaya Shibuya-ku
Tokyo 1510051   JAPAN

phone/+81-3-5414-6443
fax/+81-3-5414-6444
email/mmorioka@tohokudesign.co.jp
http://www.tohokudesign.co.jp

Mayumi Morioka

8 Write your business card. Have similar phone conversations.

company name

your name

address

phone number   fax number

email

5 It's my life! *miros*

Sports, food, and drinks · Present Simple – *I/you/they* · *a/an* · Languages and nationalities · Numbers and prices

STARTER

1 Match the words and pictures.

Sports	**Food**	**Drinks**
☐1 tennis ✓	☐ Italian food ✓	☐ tea ✓
☐8 football ✗	☐ Chinese food ✓	☐10 coffee ✓
☐14 swimming ✓	☐2 pizza ✓	☐ Coca-Cola ✓
☐7 skiing ✓	☐3 hamburgers ✓	☐9 beer ✓
	☐ oranges ✓	☐ wine ✓
	☐5 ice-cream ✓	

T 5.1 Listen and repeat.

2 Tick (✓) the things you like. Cross (✗) the things you don't like.

I don't like

THINGS I LIKE

Present Simple – *I/you*

1 **T 5.2** Listen and repeat.

I like tennis. I don't like football.

I like pizza. I don't like hamburgers.

GRAMMAR SPOT

Positive	I **like** tennis.
Negative	I **don't like** football.
	don't = do not

2 **T 5.3** Listen to Bill. Complete the sentences.

I like __swimming__ , *fut* , *are* , *pizza* , *italian* *food* , and *tennis* *beer* . *coffee*

I don't like __tennis__ , _____ , and _____ .

3 Talk to a partner about the sports, food, and drinks on p32.

I like tennis, but I don't like football.

I don't like chinese food

Questions

4 **T 5.4** Listen and repeat.

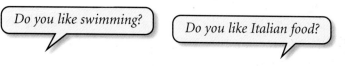

Do you like tennis?
Yes, I do.

Do you like football?
No, I don't.

GRAMMAR SPOT

Positive	I **like** . . .
Question	**Do** you **like** . . . ?
Short answers	Yes, I do. No, I don't.
▶▶ **Grammar Reference 5.1 p123**	

5 Ask your teacher about the sports, food, and drinks.

Do you like swimming?

Do you like Italian food?

6 Ask and answer the questions with a partner.

Do you like tennis?

Yes, I do. Do **you** like tennis?

No, I don't.

Bill

Reading and listening

1 **T 5.5** Read and listen to the text.

GORDON WILSON
from Aberdeen

" Hello! My name's Gordon Wilson. I come from Aberdeen in Scotland, but now I live and work in London. I have a very small flat near the centre. I'm a waiter and I'm also a drama student. I work in an Italian restaurant. I eat Italian food and I drink Italian and French wine. I don't drink beer. I don't like it. And I don't play sports. I speak three languages – English, French, and a little Italian. I want to be an actor. "

GRAMMAR SPOT

a small flat	**an** actor
a waiter	**an** Italian restaurant

▶▶ **Grammar Reference 5.2 and 5.3 p123**

---

2 **T 5.6** Listen and repeat the questions.

Questions	**Answers**
1 Do you come from Scotland?	Yes, I _do_ .
2 Do you live in Aberdeen?	No, I _don't_ . I _live_ in London.
3 Do you live in a flat?	Yes, I _do_ . I _live_ in a flat near the centre.
4 Do you work in a Chinese restaurant?	No, I _don't_ . I _work_ in an Italian restaurant.
5 Do you like Italian food?	Yes, I _do_ . I _eat_ it a lot.
6 Do you like your job?	No, I _don't_ . I want to be _an actor. - here_
7 Do you drink beer?	No, I _don't_ . I _don't_ like it.
8 Do you speak French and Spanish?	I _speak_ French but I _don't_ speak Spanish.

Complete the conversation.

T 5.7 Listen and check.

3 Ask and answer the questions with a partner. Give true answers.

Talking about you

4 **T 5.8** Listen and repeat the questions. Write about you.

1 Where do you live? (house or flat?)	I live in a _____.
2 What's your job?	I'm a/an _____.
3 Where do you work?	I work in _____.
4 What sports do you like?	I like _____.
5 What drinks do you like?	I like _____.
6 How many languages do you speak?	I speak ____ languages – _____.

Ask and answer the questions with a partner.

Roleplay

5 Work in pairs. Read the role card from your teacher. Ask and answer questions.

What . . . ?
How do you spell it?
Where . . . *do you* live?
Do . . . live in . . . ?
What . . . ?
Where . . . work?
How many . . . speak?
What sports . . . like?

... *about you*

Name	MARIO BELLINI
Town, country	MILANO ITALY
A house or a flat	FLAT
Job	A DOCTOR
Place of work	HOSPITA
Languages	ITALIA FR ENGLISH
Sports	SKIING AND TENNIS

Check it

6 Tick (✓) the correct sentence.

1 ☐ Live you in Berlin?
  ☑ Do you live in Berlin?

2 ☑ Where do you come from? *do you come from* Kana
  ☐ Where you come from?

3 ☑ Do you speak French?
  ☐ Are you speak French?

4 ☑ I don't speak French.
  ☐ I no speak French.

5 ☐ 'Do you like football?' 'Yes, I like.'
  ☑ 'Do you like football?' 'Yes, I do.'

6 ☐ 'Are you married?' 'No, I don't.'
  ☑ 'Are you married?' 'No, I'm not.'

7 ☐ He's a actor.
  ☑ He's an actor.

vowes

VOCABULARY AND PRONUNCIATION

Languages and nationalities

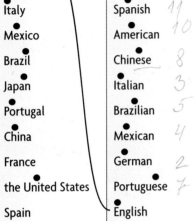

1 Match the countries and nationalities.

T 5.9 Listen, check, and repeat.

1	England	Japanese	6
2	Germany	French	9
3	Italy	Spanish	11
4	Mexico	American	10
5	Brazil	Chinese	8
6	Japan	Italian	3
7	Portugal	Brazilian	5
8	China	Mexican	4
9	France	German	2
10	the United States	Portuguese	7
11	Spain	English	

2 What nationality are the people in the pictures, do you think?

> *I think they're Italian.*

> *I think they're Spanish.*

POLAND - POLISH SLOVAKIA - SLOVAKIA

3 Make true sentences.

1	In Brazil		German.	4
2	In Canada		Italian.	5
3	In France		Japanese.	6
4	In Germany		Portuguese.	8
5	In Italy	they speak	Spanish.	7,9
6	In Japan		English.	2,2
7	In Mexico		French.	2,3
8	In Portugal			
9	In Spain			
10	In Switzerland			
11	In the United States			

T 5.10 Listen and check.

4 Practise the question. Ask and answer questions with a partner.

> *What do they speak in Brazil?*

> *Portuguese.*

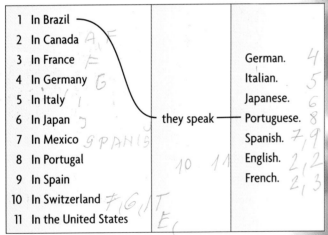

I don't like it.

5 Write the nationality.

1 an American car

2 _____ beer

GERMAN

3 SPANISH oranges

4 a _____ camera

JAPANESE

5 MEXICAN food

6 an _____ dictionary

ENGLISH

7 an _____ bag

ITALIAN

8 _____ coffee

BRAZILIAN

9 _____ wine

FRENCH

T 5.11 Listen and check.

▶▶ **Grammar Reference 5.3 p123**

6 Write sentences about you. Use the verbs *have*, *eat*, and *drink*.
I drink French wine, but I don't drink German beer.

7 Write questions. Ask and answer with a partner.

Do you have an American car?   *Yes, I do.*   *No, I don't. I have a German car.*

Do you drink German beer?   *Yes, I do.*   *No, I don't. I don't drink beer. I don't like it.*

LISTENING AND SPEAKING

At a party

1 **T 5.12** Alessandra and Woody are at a party in London.
Listen to the conversation. Tick (✓) what Woody says.

1 ✓ I work in London.
☐ I don't work in London.
2 ☐ I live in London.
✓ I live in Brighton. *a*
3 ✓ I'm an actor.
☐ I'm a doctor.
4 ☐ You don't speak English very well.
✓ You speak English very well.
5 ✓ I like Italy.
✓ I love Italy.
6 ✓ I like the food and the wine very much.
☐ I don't like the food and the wine very much.

2 Practise the conversation. Look at the tapescript on p114.

Roleplay

3 You are at a party in London. Think of a new identity.
Complete the role card. *rola, herecká úloha*

Name:	*John*	Job:	*a doctor*
Work in:	*hospital*	Live in:	*where Zimbabve*
Speak:	*2*	Like:	*tea, dzus, still water*

Hello. I'm _____.

Hi. I'm _____.

Do you live here?

4 Stand up. Talk to people at the party.

EVERYDAY ENGLISH

Numbers and prices

1 Count from 1–30 round the class.

2 **T 5.13** Listen and repeat.

10 ten
20 twenty
30 thirty
40 forty
50 fifty
60 sixty
70 seventy
80 eighty
90 ninety
100 one hundred

Count to 100 in tens round the class.

3 Work with a partner.

Student A
Write some numbers.
Say them to your partner.

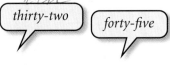

thirty-two   *forty-five*

Student B
Write the numbers you hear.
32 45 ...

4 **T 5.14** Read and listen to the prices.
Practise them.

30p	thirty p /piː/
50p	fifty p
75p	seventy-five p
£1	one pound
£20	twenty pounds
£75	seventy-five pounds
£1.60	one pound sixty
£3.45	three pounds forty-five
£22.80	twenty-two pounds eighty

5 Say the prices.

60p	97p	£17	£70	£25
£1.50	£16.80	£40.75	£26.99	

T 5.15 Listen and check.

6 **T 5.16** Listen and tick (✓) the prices you hear.

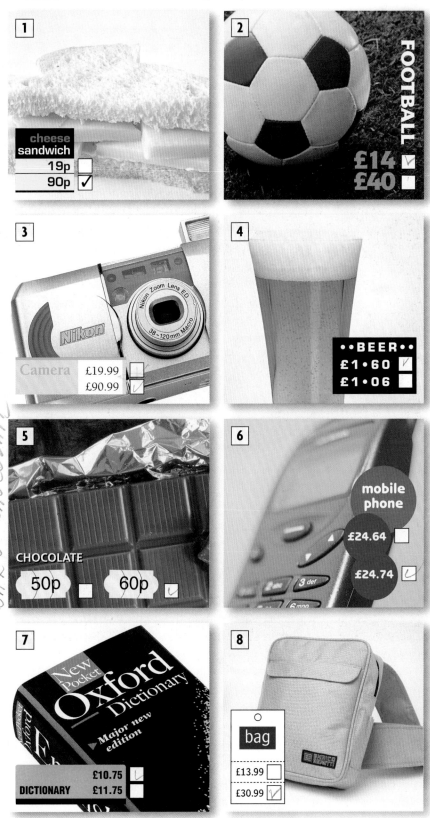

7 Ask and answer questions about the pictures with a partner.

How much is the cheese sandwich?

It's 90p.

6 Every day

STARTER

1 **T 6.1** Listen and repeat. Write the times.

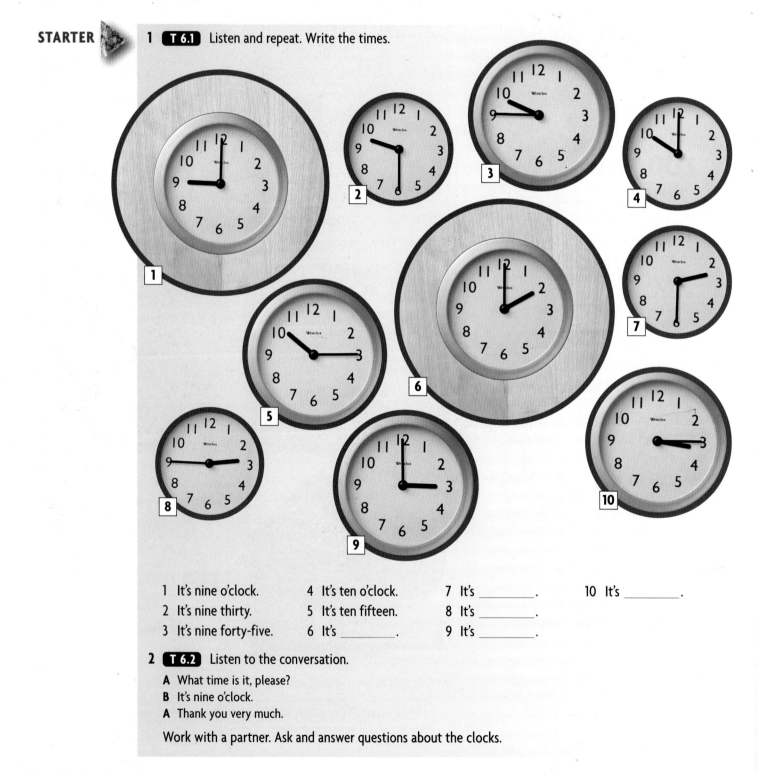

1 It's nine o'clock.   4 It's ten o'clock.   7 It's _____.   10 It's _____.

2 It's nine thirty.   5 It's ten fifteen.   8 It's _____.

3 It's nine forty-five.   6 It's _____.   9 It's _____.

2 **T 6.2** Listen to the conversation.

A What time is it, please?

B It's nine o'clock.

A Thank you very much.

Work with a partner. Ask and answer questions about the clocks.

WHAT TIME DO YOU . . . ?
Present Simple – *I/you*

1 **T 6.3** Listen to Lena talking about her schooldays. Circle the times.

1 I get up at 7.30 / 7.45

2 I have breakfast at 8.00 / 8.15

3 I go to school at 8.30 / 8.40

4 I have lunch at 12.15 / 12.45

5 I leave school at 3.30 / 4.15

6 I get home at 4.30 / 4.45

7 I go to bed at 11.00 / 11.30

T 6.3 Listen and check. Practise the sentences.

2 Talk to a partner about your day.

> *I get up at seven thirty. I have breakfast at …*

3 **T 6.4** Listen and repeat the questions.

What time do you get up?
What time do you have breakfast?

Work with another partner. Ask and answer questions about your day.

> *What time do you go to work?*

> *I go to work at 8.15.*

KARL'S DAY

Present Simple – *he / she / it*, *usually / sometimes / never*

1 Karl Wilk is 22 and he is a computer millionaire. He's the director of **netstore24.com**, a 24-hour shopping site on the Internet.

Read about his day. Look at the pictures. Write the times.

1 He <u>gets up</u> at <u>six o'clock</u> and he <u>has</u> a shower.

2 He has breakfast at *6.45*.

3 He leaves home at *7.15* and he goes to work by taxi.

4 He has lunch (a Coca-Cola and a sandwich) in his office at *1.PM*.

5 He usually works late. He leaves work at *8 p.m* in the evening.

6 He sometimes buys a pizza and eats it at home. He gets home at *9.15 15k nine*.

7 He never goes out in the evening. He works at his computer from *9.30* to *11.30 p.m*.

8 He goes to bed at *11.45 p.m*.

GRAMMAR SPOT

1 <u>Underline</u> the verbs in 1–8.
<u>gets up</u>   <u>has</u>
What is the last letter?
T 6.5 Listen and repeat.

2 Look at the adverbs of frequency.

90%	40%	0%
usually	sometimes	never

Find *usually*, *sometimes*, *never* in 1–8.
T 6.6 Listen and repeat.

▶▶ **Grammar Reference 6.1–6.3 p124**

1 6:00 AM

2 6:45 AM

4 1:00 PM

5 8:00 PM

7 9:30 PM   11:30 PM

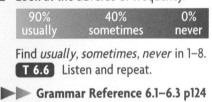

netstore24.com

7:15 AM

11:45 PM

Questions and negatives

2 Read the questions. Complete the answers.

1 What time does he get up?	He _____ up at 6.00.
2 When does he go to bed?	He _gets_ to bed at 11.45.
3 Does he go to work by taxi?	_yes_, he does.
4 Does he have lunch in a restaurant?	_no_, he doesn't.
5 Does he go out in the evening?	No, he _____.

T 6.7 Listen, check, and repeat. Practise the questions and answers.

> **GRAMMAR SPOT**
>
> **1**   He get**s** up early.
>   What time **does** he get up?
>   He **doesn't** get up late.   *doesn't* = does not
> **2** Does he get up early?   **Yes, he does.**
>   Does he have lunch at home?   **No, he doesn't.**
>   These are short answers.

3 Work with a partner. Ask and answer questions about Karl's day.

> *What time does he have breakfast?*

> *He has breakfast at 6.45.*

Ask and answer about these things.

1 What time/have breakfast?
2 When/leave home?
3 Does/go to work by bus?
4 Where/have lunch?

5 Does/usually work late?
6 Does/eat in a restaurant?
7 What/do in the evening?

T 6.8 Listen and check.

> **GRAMMAR SPOT**
>
> **1** Complete the table for the Present Simple.
>
> | | Positive | Negative |
> |---|---|---|
> | I | work | don't work |
> | You | | |
> | He | | |
> | She | works | doesn't work |
> | We | | |
> | They | | |
>
> **2** Complete the questions.
>   1 When _____ you get up?   2 When _____ he get up?
>
> ▶▶ **Grammar Reference 6.4 p124**

PRACTICE

Katya's day

1 Karl has a sister, Katya. Her day is different. Complete the text with the verbs.

gets	gets up x2	has	paints	drinks
cooks	listens to	goes x2	plays	~~lives~~

Katya is 25.
She's an artist.

She _lives_ in a small house in the country. She usually _gets up_ at ten o'clock in the morning. She never _gets_ early. She _has_ coffee and toast for breakfast and then she _goes_ for a walk with her dog. She _goes_ home at eleven o'clock and she _paints_ in her studio until seven o'clock in the evening. Then she _cooks_ dinner and _drinks_ a glass of wine. After dinner, she sometimes _listens to_ music and she sometimes _plays_ the piano. She usually _goes_ to bed very late, at one or two o'clock in the morning.

T 6.9 Listen and check.

2 Is the sentence about Karl or Katya? Write *he* or *she*.

1 _He_ 's a millionaire.
2 _She_ 's an artist.
3 _____ lives in the country.
4 _____ doesn't have a dog.
5 _____ gets up very early.
6 _____ works at home in a studio.
7 _____ doesn't work in an office.
8 _____ doesn't cook.
9 _____ likes wine.
10 _____ loves computers.

Practise the sentences.

Negatives and pronunciation

3 Correct the sentences about Katya and Karl.

1 She lives in the town.

She doesn't live in the town. She lives in the country.

2 He gets up at ten o'clock.

_____

3 She has a big breakfast.

_____

4 He has a dog.

_____

5 She works in an office.

_____

6 He cooks dinner in the evening.

_____

7 She goes to bed early.

_____

8 They go out in the evening.

_____

T 6.10 Listen, check, and repeat.

Talking about you

4 Work with a partner. Write the names of two people in your family. Ask and answer questions about them.

- Who is . . . ?
- How old is . . . ?
- What's . . . job?
- Where does . . . live?
- Where does . . . work?
- What time does she/he . . . ?
- Does she/he have . . . ?

Maria

alfonso

Who is she?   *She's my sister.*

Who is he?   *He's my grandfather.*

Check it

5 Complete the questions and answers with *do, don't, does,* or *doesn't.*

1 '_____ you like ice-cream?'   'Yes, I _____.'
2 '_____ she work in London?'   'Yes, she _____.'
3 'Where _____ he work?'   'In a bank.'
4 '_____ you go to work by bus?'   'No, I _____.'
5 '_____ she go to bed early?'   'No, she _____.'
6 '_____ they have a dog?'   'Yes, they _____.'
7 '_____ he speak German?'   'No, he _____.'
8 '_____ they live in the United States?'   'No, they _____.'

VOCABULARY AND SPEAKING

Words that go together

1 Match a verb in **A** with a line in **B**.

A	B
get up	dinner
go	early
listen to	TV
watch	in an office
cook	music
work	to bed late

A	B
go	in restaurants
have	the piano
eat	beer
drink	shopping
play	at home
stay	a shower

T 6.11 Listen and check.

2 **T 6.12** Look at the questionnaire. Listen and practise the questions.

3 Ask a partner the questions and complete the questionnaire. Tick (✓) the correct column.

Do you get up early?

Yes, usually.

Yes, sometimes.

No, never.

4 Tell the class about you and your partner.

*Juan usually gets up early.
I never get up early.*

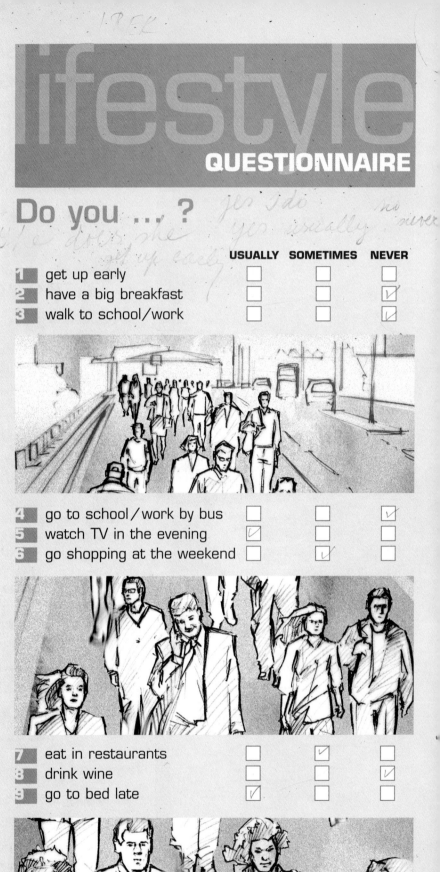

lifestyle
QUESTIONNAIRE

Do you ... ?

		USUALLY	SOMETIMES	NEVER
1	get up early	☐	☐	☐
2	have a big breakfast	☐	☐	✓
3	walk to school/work	☐	☐	✓
4	go to school/work by bus	☐	☐	✓
5	watch TV in the evening	✓	☐	☐
6	go shopping at the weekend	☐	✓	☐
7	eat in restaurants	☐	✓	☐
8	drink wine	☐	☐	✓
9	go to bed late	✓	☐	☐

EVERYDAY ENGLISH

Days of the week

1 **T 6.13** Listen and order the days.

Wednesday	Friday	Tuesday	Saturday	Thursday

1	2	3	4	5	6	7
Monday	Tuesday	Wednesday	Thursday	Friday	Saturday	Sunday

T 6.13 Listen again and repeat. Practise the days.

2 Answer the questions.

1 What day is it today?
2 What day is it tomorrow?
3 What days do you go to school/work?
4 What days are the weekend?
5 What days do you like?
6 What days don't you like?

3 Write the correct preposition in the boxes.

in	on	at

Sunday
Monday
Tuesday
Saturday evening
Thursday morning
Friday afternoon

nine o'clock
[at] ten thirty
twelve fifteen
the weekend

[on]

[in] the morning
the afternoon
the evening

T 6.14 Listen and check.

4 Write the correct preposition. Then answer the questions.

Do you have English lessons . . .

1 _at_ nine o'clock?
2 _on_ Sunday?
3 _in_ the evening?
4 _on_ Monday morning?
5 _at_ the weekend?

Yes, we do.

No, we don't.

When do you have English lessons?

We have English lessons . . .

5 Complete the questions. Ask and answer them with a partner.

Do you . . .

- have a shower . . . _in_ the morning/evening?
- get up early . . . _on_ Sunday morning?
- go to work/school . . . _on_ Saturday?
- eat in restaurants . . . _at_ the weekend?
- watch TV . . . _in_ the afternoon?
- stay at home . . . _on_ Friday evening?

7 Places I like

Question words · it/them · this/that · Adjectives · Can I ... ?

STARTER

1 Match the questions and answers.

	A	B
1	What is the capital of Australia?	4,500 years old.
2	How old are the Pyramids?	86. It is
3	What time do Spanish people have dinner?	$3.50.
4	Where does the American President live?	The Queen of England.
5	How many floors does the Empire State Building have?	In the White House.
6	How much is a hamburger in the US?	Canberra.
7	Who lives in Buckingham Palace?	Late. At 10.00 in the evening.

T 7.1 Listen and check.

2 What is your favourite town or city? Why do you like it?

I LOVE IT HERE!

it/them, this/that

1 **T 7.2** Listen and complete the conversation on p49. Use these words.

why because me you him it them

2 Practise the conversation with a partner.

3 Complete the questions and answers.

1 Why **does** Céline live in London? Because she _likes_ it in England.
2 Does she like English people? Yes, she loves _them_.
3 How _many_ children does she have? Three.
4 Where _does_ her sons go to school? In England.
5 _Why_ does Lisa-Marie go to school in the US? _because_ she lives with her father.

GRAMMAR SPOT

1 Underline the question words in the *Starter*. _What_ _How old_
2 Complete the table. _my your his her Its our their_

Subject pronoun	I	you	he	she	it	we	they
Object pronoun	me	you	him	her	it	us	them

3 Find examples of *this* and *that* in the conversation with Céline. _them_

▶▶ **Grammar Reference 7.1–7.3 p124**

---

predmet

CÉLINE, THE FAMOUS HOLLYWOOD FILM STAR, IS IN HER HOUSE IN LONDON. SHE IS WITH GUY NORMAN, A JOURNALIST.

Guy: This is a very beautiful house.

Céline: Thank you. I like it very much, too.

Guy: Céline, you're American. Why do you live here in London?

Céline: Because I just love _it_ here! The people are fantastic! I love them! And of course, my husband, Charles, is English, and I love him, too!

Guy: That's a very nice photo. Who are they?

Céline: My sons. That's Matt, and that's Jack. They go to school here. My daughter's at school in the US. Her name's Lisa-Marie.

Guy: _Why_ does Lisa-Marie go to school in the US?

Céline: _because_ she lives with her father. My first husband, you know, the actor Dan Brat. I hate _him_ and all his movies. I never watch _them_.

Guy: I see. And does Lisa-Marie visit you?

Céline: Oh, yes. She visits me every vacation. She's here with _me_ now.

Guy: And is this a photo of _you_ and Charles?

Céline: Oh yes. It's us in Hawaii. It's our wedding. We're so happy together!

THAT

THIS

1 Look at the picture. Ask and answer questions.

What's this?

It's a phone.

What's that?

It's a dog.

2 Ask and answer questions about things in your classroom.

What's that?

It's Martha's bag.

What's this?

It's a book.

What is that?

I don't know.

I like them!

3 Complete the sentences with an object pronoun.

1 Do you like ice-cream?
Yes, I love __it__ .

2 Do you like dogs?
No, I hate _____ .

3 Do you like me?
Of course I like _you_ !

4 Does your teacher teach you French?
No, she teaches _us_ English.

5 Do you like your teacher?
We like _____ very much.

T 7.3 Listen and check.

What do you like?

4 Ask and answer questions with a partner.
Ask about …

football

holidays

your sister/brother

television

rock music

cats

chocolate

mobile phones

computers

dogs

Do you like football?

Yes, I do. I love it.

No, I don't. I hate it.

It's all right.

Questions and answers

5 Work with a partner. Ask and answer the questions.

1 Why/Céline drink champagne?   (… like …)
Why does Céline drink champagne?   **Because she likes it.**

2 Why/you/eat oranges?   (… like …)
_____   _____

3 Why/Annie want to marry Peter?   (… love …)
_____   _____

4 Why/you eat Chinese food?   (… like …)
_____   _____

5 Why/not like your maths teacher?   (… give … a lot of homework.)
_____   _____

6 Why/Miguel buy presents for Maria? (… love …)
_____   _____

T 7.4 Listen and check.

6 Match the questions and answers.

1 How do you come to school?
2 What do you have for breakfast?
3 Who is your favourite pop group?
4 Where does your father work?
5 Why do you want to learn English?
6 How much money do you have in your bag?
7 When do lessons start at your school?
8 How many languages does your teacher speak?

They start at nine o'clock.
In an office in the centre of town.
Three.
Not a lot. About two pounds.
I don't have a favourite. I like a lot.
By bus.
Because it's an international language.
Toast and coffee.

T 7.5 Listen and check. Practise the questions.

Work with a partner. Ask and answer the questions about you.

Check it

7 Tick (✓) the correct sentence.

1 ☐ What do you do at the weekend?
  ☐ Where do you do at the weekend?

2 ☐ Who is your boyfriend?
  ☐ When is your boyfriend?

3 ☐ How many money do you have?
  ☐ How much money do you have?

4 ☐ I don't drink beer. I don't like.
  ☐ I don't drink beer. I don't like it.

5 ☐ Our teacher gives us a lot of homework.
  ☐ Our teacher gives we a lot of homework.

6 ☐ She loves me and I love her.
  ☐ She loves my and I love she.

VOCABULARY

Adjectives

1 Match the words and pictures. Write sentences.

new   expensive   lovely   small   old   horrible   hot   cold   cheap   ~~big~~

1 It's lovely.

2 horrible

3 old

4 new

5 big

6 small

7 hot

8 cold

9 expensive

10 cheap

T 7.6 Listen and check. Practise the sentences.

2 Write the opposite adjectives.

Adjective	new	expensive	lovely	small	cold
Opposite	old	cheap	horrib	big	hot

READING AND WRITING

A postcard from Dublin

1 **T 7.7** Look at the postcard. Read and listen. Check the meaning of new words.

Dear Alan

We're on holiday in Dublin this week. Our hotel is very nice – old and comfortable. The people are very friendly, and the food is delicious.

Irish music is good, and the beer is lovely!

Dublin is beautiful. It's a big city, with a lot of old buildings, and it isn't expensive.

The weather is horrible! It's wet and it's cold!

See you soon.

Love
Dona and Sergio
(your Italian students!)

IRELAND

Alan Bates

The English School

Viale Carso 44-46

00195 Rome

ITALY

Photography: Peter O'Toole. 2/GL 15
Printed and Published in Ireland by John Hinde Ltd. ©

2 Answer the questions.
  1 Who is the postcard from?
  2 Where are they?
  3 Why are they in Dublin?
  4 Is their holiday good?
  5 What isn't good?

3 What adjectives do Dona and Sergio use? Complete the chart.

	Adjectives
their hotel	nice, old, comfortable
Irish people	FRIENDLY
the food	DELICIOUS
Irish music	good
the beer	LOVELY
Dublin	Beautiful, Big, expensive, old
the weather	horrible, cold

4 Write a postcard to a friend.

Dear ...
We're on holiday in ... and it's very ...
Our hotel is ...   The people are ...
The food is ... and the wine is ...
The weather ... hot, and ... to the beach every day.
See you soon,   Love ...

EVERYDAY ENGLISH

Can I . . . ?

1 Write a number 1–5 (place) and a letter a–e (activity) for each picture.

PLACES	ACTIVITIES
+ a railway station	a try on a jumper
2 a café	b change a traveller's cheque
3 a bank	c have a ham sandwich
4 an Internet café	~~d~~ buy a return ticket
5 a clothes shop	e send an email

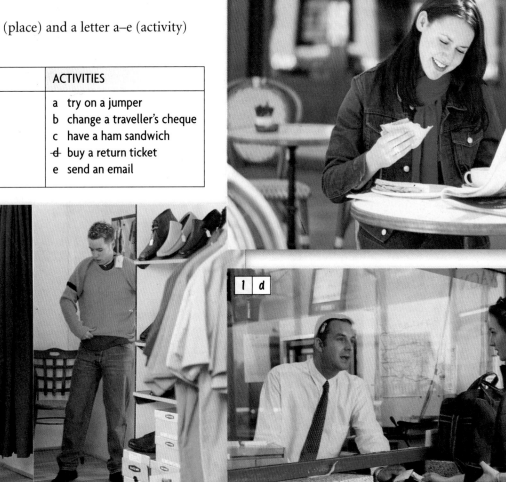

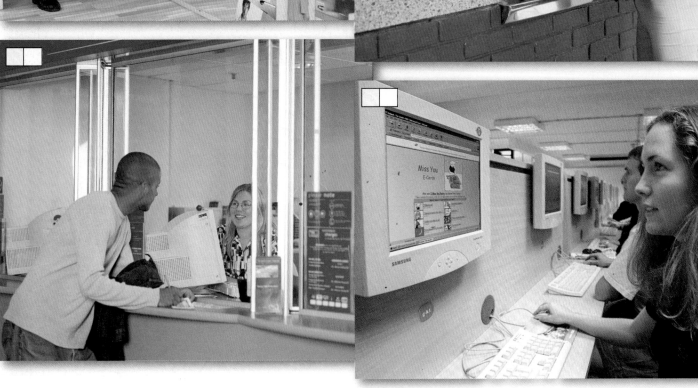

2 **T 7.8** Listen to Keiko. She is in different places in town. Where is she in the conversations? What does she want? Choose from exercise 1.

Where is she?	What does she want?
1 In a café.	To have a ham sandwich.
2 a Clothes shop	SHE try on this jumper
3 an Internet café	SHE SENDS THE email
4 a bank	SHE WANTS CHANGE TRAVELLER'S cheque
5 a STATION	SHE WANTS buy a TICKET TO...

3 Complete the conversations with a partner.

1 A Yes, please!
  K Can I have _A HAM SANDW_, please?
  A OK.
  K How _MUCH_ is that?
  A _2 POUNDS_ ninety, please.
  K There you are.
  A Thanks _A LOT_.

2 K Hello. Can I _TRY ON_ this jumper, please?
  B _OF COURSE_. The changing rooms are just here.

3 K _CAN I SEND AN_ email, please?
  C OK. PC _NUMBER 2_.
  K _HOW MUCH_ is it?
  C 1p a minute. Pay at the end, please.

4 D Good morning. Can I help you?
  K Yes, please. _CAN I CHANGE_ this traveller's cheque?
  D How much is it?
  K _50_ dollars.
  D OK.

5 K _CAN I BUY_ a return ticket to Oxford, please?
  E Sure.
  K How much _IS THAT_?
  E Twenty-two _150_, please.
  K Thank you.
  E Twenty-five pounds. Here's _YOUR TICKET_, and £2.50 change.

T 7.8 Listen and check.

Practise the conversations.

4 Work with a partner. Make more conversations with different information.

Student A	Student B
• a coffee	• an ice-cream
• this jacket	• this T-shirt
• a return ticket to Edinburgh	• a single ticket to Manchester

8 Where I live

STARTER

1 Do you live in a house or a flat? Do you have a garden? Tell the class.

I live in a flat.

We don't have a garden.

2 **T 8.1** Look at the picture. Listen and repeat the rooms of a house.

living room, dining room . . .

3 Find the things in the house. Write the numbers.

| ☐ 1 a bed | ☐ 12 a cooker | ☐ 9 a sofa | ☐ 4 a TV | ☐ 3 a shower | ☐ a table |
| ☐ 6 a CD player | ☐ 7 an armchair | ☐ 2 a lamp | ☐ 11 a picture | ☐ 8 a magazine | ☐ a video recorder |

T 8.2 Listen and repeat.

NICOLE'S LIVING ROOM
There is / are, any

1 **T 8.3** Read and listen to Nicole describing her living room. Complete the sentences.

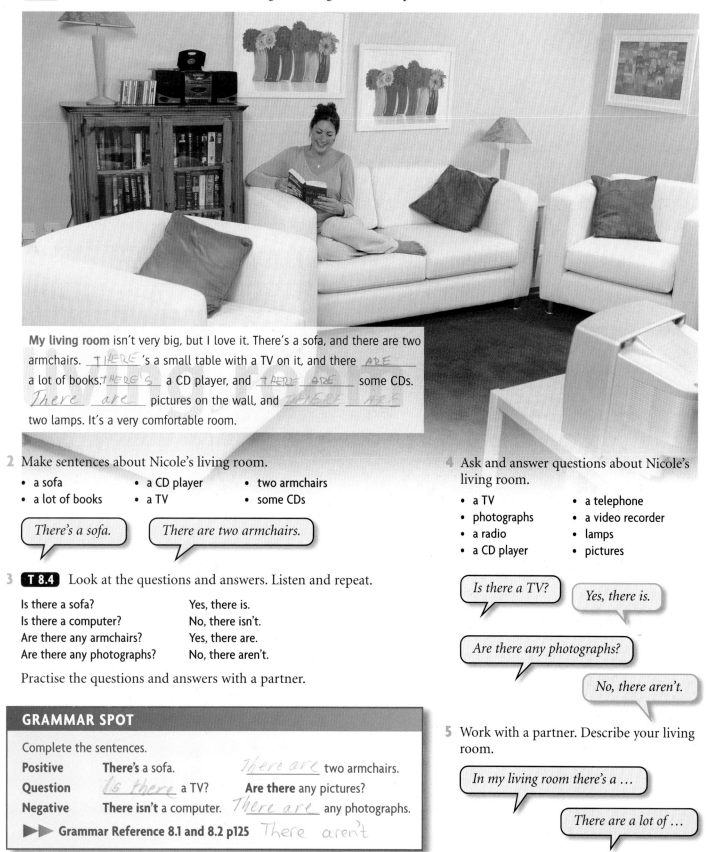

My living room isn't very big, but I love it. There's a sofa, and there are two armchairs. ___THERE___'s a small table with a TV on it, and there ___ARE___ a lot of books. ___THERE'S___ a CD player, and ___THERE ARE___ some CDs. ___There are___ pictures on the wall, and ___THERE ARE___ two lamps. It's a very comfortable room.

2 Make sentences about Nicole's living room.

- a sofa
- a CD player
- two armchairs
- a lot of books
- a TV
- some CDs

> *There's a sofa.*

> *There are two armchairs.*

3 **T 8.4** Look at the questions and answers. Listen and repeat.

Is there a sofa?   Yes, there is.
Is there a computer?   No, there isn't.
Are there any armchairs?   Yes, there are.
Are there any photographs? No, there aren't.

Practise the questions and answers with a partner.

GRAMMAR SPOT

Complete the sentences.

Positive	There's a sofa.	*There are* two armchairs.
Question	*Is there* a TV?	**Are there** any pictures?
Negative	**There isn't** a computer.	*There are* any photographs. *There aren't*

▶▶ Grammar Reference 8.1 and 8.2 p125

---

4 Ask and answer questions about Nicole's living room.

- a TV
- photographs
- a radio
- a CD player
- a telephone
- a video recorder
- lamps
- pictures

> *Is there a TV?*

> *Yes, there is.*

> *Are there any photographs?*

> *No, there aren't.*

5 Work with a partner. Describe your living room.

> *In my living room there's a …*

> *There are a lot of …*

NICOLE'S BEDROOM
Prepositions

1 Look at the prepositions.   *predložka*

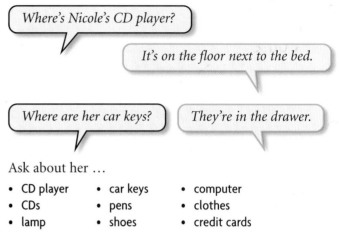

in   on   under   next to

2 Look at Nicole's bedroom. Write a preposition from exercise 1.

1 Nicole's mobile phone is __on__ the bed.
2 The magazine is __NEXT TO__ the phone.
3 Her CD player is __ON__ the floor __NEXT TO__ the bed.
4 Her car keys are __IN__ the drawer.
5 Her bag is __ON__ the floor __UNDER__ the chair.
6 The books are __UNDER__ her bed.

T 8.5 Listen and check. Practise the sentences.

3 Ask and answer questions about Nicole's things.

> *Where's Nicole's CD player?*

> *It's on the floor next to the bed.*

> *Where are her car keys?*   *They're in the drawer.*

Ask about her …

- CD player
- CDs
- lamp
- car keys
- pens
- shoes
- computer
- clothes
- credit cards

4 Close your eyes! Ask and answer questions about things in your classroom.

> *Where is Juan's dictionary?*   *It's in his bag.*

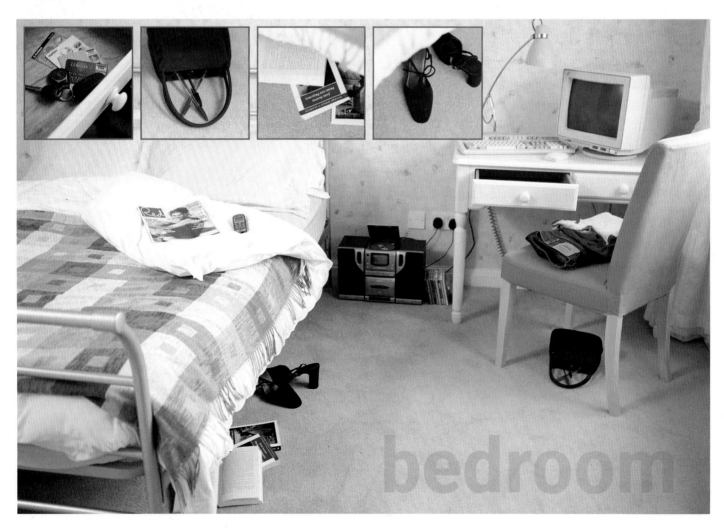

PRACTICE

Questions and answers

1 Put the words in the correct order to make a question.

1 house live or in you a Do flat a

Do you live in a house or a flat ?

2 bedrooms How many there are

HOW MANY BEDROOMS ARE THERE?

3 telephone the Is there kitchen a in

THERE IS IN THE KITCHEN TELEPHONE?

4 living room a the there Is in television

THERE IS IN THE LIVING ROOM A TELEVISION?

5 the a Is video recorder there television under

THERE IS THE VIDEO RECORDER UNDER TELEVISION?

6 Are in your books bedroom there a lot of

ARE THERE A LOT OF BOOKS IN YOUR BEDROOM?

7 pictures there Are wall on the any

ARE THERE ANY PICTURES ON THE WALL?

T 8.6 Listen and check.

2 Work with a partner. Ask and answer the questions about where you live.

Different rooms

3 Work with a partner.

Student A Look at the picture below.
Student B Look at the picture on p139.

Your pictures are different. Talk about your pictures to find six differences.

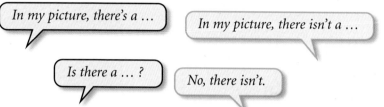

In my picture, there's a …

In my picture, there isn't a …

Is there a … ?

No, there isn't.

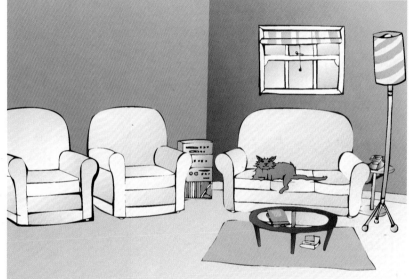

4 **T 8.7** Listen to a description of one of the rooms. Which room is it?

Check it

5 Tick (✓) the correct sentence.

1 ☐ Is a sofa in the living room?
   ☑ Is there a sofa in the living room?

2 ☑ There's a CD player.
   ☐ There are a CD player.

3 ☐ Are there a lamps?
   ☑ Are there any lamps?

4 ☑ Your keys are in the drawer.
   ☐ Your keys are on the drawer.

5 ☑ The lamp is next to the bed.
   ☐ The lamp is next the bed.

READING AND SPEAKING
Sydney

1 Look at the pictures of Sydney, Australia. Find these things in the pictures.

- the Opera House
- a beach
- a harbour
- a ferry
- windsurfing
- sailing
- a bridge
- a park

2 Read the text about Sydney on p61. Here are the five paragraph headings. Write them in the correct place.

What to do

What to eat

Where to stay

When to go

How to travel

T 8.8 Listen and check.

3 Complete the chart with an adjective or a noun from the text.

Adjective	Noun
old / new	buildings
fantastic	beaches
delicious	food
cheap	hotels in King's Cross
expensive	hotels in the centre
~~Pitt Street~~	shops
	bridge
famous	Bondi Beach
fresh	seafood
fast	trains
	buses

4 Answer the questions.

1 When are the best times to go?
2 Are all the hotels expensive?
3 What do people do … ?
   - in Pitt Street
   - at the beach
   - in Oxford Street
4 What restaurants are there in Sydney?
5 What is the best way to see Sydney?

how to have a good time in ...
Sydney

Sydney has everything you want in a city. It's beautiful, it has old and new buildings, there are fantastic beaches, and the food is delicious.

WHEN TO GO

The best times to visit are spring and autumn. In summer it is very hot.

WHERE TO STAY

There are cheap hotels in King's Cross. A room is about $50 a night. There are international hotels in the centre. Here a room is about $150 a night.

WHAT TO DO

Sydney has theatres and cinemas, and of course, the Opera House. The best shops are in Pitt Street.

Go to the harbour. There are beaches, walks, parks, and cafés and, of course, the wonderful bridge.

Sydney has the famous Bondi Beach. People go swimming, surfing, windsurfing, and sailing.

For night-life, there are clubs and bars in Oxford Street.

WHAT TO EAT

There are restaurants from every country – Italian, Turkish, Lebanese, Japanese, Thai, Chinese, and Vietnamese. Australians eat a lot of seafood – it's very fresh!

HOW TO TRAVEL

There are fast trains and slow buses. The best way to see Sydney is by ferry.

LISTENING AND WRITING

My home town

1 **T 8.9** Listen to Darren. He lives in Sydney. Tick (✓) the things he talks about. Listen again. What does he say about them?

sailing	☐	_____
his brother	✓	He lives in a house with his brother.
surfing	☐	_____
train	☐	_____
cinema	☐	_____
the Harbour	☐	_____
the Opera House	☐	_____
seafood	☐	_____
his girlfriend	☐	_____
Oxford Street	☐	_____
Japanese food	☐	_____
Manly Beach	☐	_____
ferry	☐	_____

2 In groups, talk about your town or a town you like.

- Where do you live?
- Where do you work/go to school?
- What do you do with your friends?
- Where do you go shopping?
- What do you do when you go out?

3 Write about a town you know. Use these paragraph headings and ideas.

What to do
There is a cinema . . . The best shops . . . Go to . . .

What to eat
There are good restaurants in . . .

Where to stay
. . . is an expensive hotel. . . . is a cheap hotel.

When to visit
The best time to visit is . . .

How to travel
The best way to travel is . . .

EVERYDAY ENGLISH

Directions

1 Find the places on the map.

bank	chemist	cinema	post office	newsagent	church	supermarket	railway station	Internet café

2 What do the signs mean?

turn right	go straight on	turn left

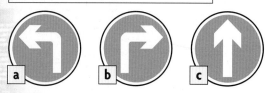

3 **T 8.10** Listen to the directions. Start from YOU ARE HERE on the map. Follow the directions. Where are you?

Go down King's Road. Turn right at the Grand Hotel into Charles Street. It's next to the cinema.

1 **At the chemist.**
2
3
4
5

Look at the tapescript on p116. Practise the conversations.

4 Work with a partner. Have similar conversations.

Ask about …
- a cinema
- a post office
- a newsagent
- a supermarket
- a theatre
- an Italian restaurant

Excuse me! Is there a … near here?

Yes. Go down …

5 Ask for and give directions in your town.

How do I get to the bus station?

Go out of the school. Turn right …

Is it far?

About ten minutes.

9 Happy birthday!

Saying years · was/were born · Past Simple – irregular verbs · When's your birthday?

STARTER

1 **T 9.1** Listen and <u>underline</u> the years you hear. Say them.

1 1426 / 1526
2 1699 / 1799
3 1818 / 1880
4 1939 / 1949
5 1951 / 1961
6 2007 / 2010

2 What year is it now? What year was it last year?

❗	We say:	**1841**	eighteen forty-one
		1916	nineteen sixteen
	but	**2000**	two thousand
		2008	two thousand and eight
		2015	two thousand and fifteen
T 9.2	Listen and repeat.		

WHEN WERE THEY BORN?

was/were born

1 **T 9.3** Do you know the people? When were they born?
Listen and write the years.

Leonardo da Vinci **painter and scientist**
born 1452 Tuscany, Italy.

Marie Curie **scientist** *vědec*
born 1867 Warsaw, Poland.

SKLODOVSKA

2 **T 9.4** Listen and repeat.

He was a painter.
He was born in 1452.

She was a scientist.
She was born in 1867.

I was born in 1979.

3 Ask and answer questions with other students.

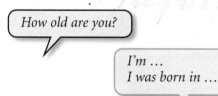

How old are you?

I'm …
I was born in …

4 **T 9.5** Listen to the questions and answers. Practise them.

When were you born?	I was born in 1986.
When was he born?	He was born in 1975.
When was she born?	She was born in 1991.
When were they born?	They were born in 2001.

GRAMMAR SPOT

Complete the table of the verb *to be*.

	Present	Past
I	am	was
You	are	*were*
He/She/It	is	*was*
We	are	were
They	are	*were*

▶▶ **Grammar Reference 9.1 p125**

5 **T 9.6** This is Calico Jones. Listen to her talking about her family. Write when they were born.

Calico Jones

Calico **1987**

Calico's family

Henry *1992*
William *1993*
Cleo *1999*
Linda *1961*
Alan *1961*
Violet *1932*

Ask and answer questions about the people.

Who's Cleo? She's Calico's sister.

When was she born? In 19…*87*

Who are Linda and Alan? They're her …*parents*

When were they …*born* Linda was born …*1961*
Alan …*1961*

6 Write the names of some people in your family. Ask and answer questions about them.

Who's Alberto? He's my grandfather.

When was he born? I think he was born in …

7 Tell the class about your partner's family.

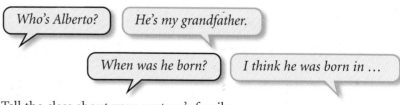

Anna's grandfather was born in 1936.
Her mother was born in 1959.

PRACTICE

Who were they?

1 Do you know the people in the photographs?
Match the people 1–8 and jobs.

5 singer	☐ musician	☐ actor
☑ writer	☑ painter	☐ princess
☐ politician	☐ racing driver	

Van Gogh
born _____,
Holland.

Beethoven
born 1770 ,
Germany.

Shakespeare
born 1564 ,
England.

T 9.7 Listen and write the year they
were born.

3 **T 9.8** Listen to the questions and
answers. Practise them.

Who was Shakespeare?   He was a writer.
Where was he born?   In England.
When was he born?   In 1564.

Ask and answer the questions about the
other people with a partner.

Who was Van Gogh?

He was a …

Marilyn Monroe
born _____,
the US.

Elvis Presley
born 1935,
the US.

6

Diana Spencer
born ~~1961~~,
England.

7

Ayrton Senna
born *racing*,
Brazil. *1960*

8

Indira Gandhi
born ~~1917~~,
India. *politician*

Negatives and pronunciation

4 **T 9.9** Listen and repeat.

Shakespeare was a painter.

No, he wasn't. He was a writer.

Shakespeare and Diana were French.

No, they weren't. They were English.

> **!**
> /wəz/
> **1** He was a painter.
> /wɒznt/
> No, he wasn't.
> *wasn't* = was not
> /wə/
> **2** They were American.
> /wɜːnt/
> No, they weren't.
> *weren't* = were not

5 Write the correct information.

1 Ayrton Senna was an actor.
  No, he WASN'T. He was a racer.

2 Marie Curie was a princess.
  No, she WASN'T.

3 Marilyn Monroe and Elvis Presley were Italian.
  No, they WEREN'T. They were American.

4 Beethoven was a scientist.
  No, he WASN'T. He was a musician.

5 Leonardo da Vinci and Van Gogh were musicians.
  No, they WEREN'T. They were painters.

6 Indira Gandhi was a singer.
  No, she WASN'T. She was politician.

T 9.10 Listen, check, and repeat. Practise the sentences.

Today and yesterday

6 What is true for you? Tell a partner.

Today is . . . *Thursday*	Monday / Tuesday / Wednesday . . .
Yesterday was . . .	
Today I'm . . . *at school*	at school / at home / at work . . .
Yesterday I was . . . *at work on holiday*	
Today the weather is . . . *cold lovely*	hot / cold / wet / lovely / horrible . . .
Yesterday the weather was . . . *cold frosty*	
Today my parents are . . . *work*	at work / at home . . .
Yesterday my parents were . . . *at home*	

Check it

7 Complete the sentences with *was*, *wasn't*, *were*, or *weren't*.

1 Where WAS your mother born?

2 When WERE your parents born?

3 No, my parents WEREN'T both born in 1951. My *father* WAS born in 1951, and my mother in 1953.

4 Yes, I WAS in New York in 1999.

5 WAS he at home yesterday? No, he WASN'T.

6 WERE you at work yesterday? Yes, we WEREN'T.

7 WERE they at school yesterday morning? No, they WEREN'T.

VOCABULARY AND READING
Past Simple – irregular verbs

1 Match the present and the past forms. Look at the irregular verb list on p142.

Present	Past
are	**was**
is	were
buy	**went**
go	**said** *SED*
say	bought
see -*so*	**took** *tuk*
take -*tuk*	saw -*so*

T 9.11 Listen, check, and repeat.

▶▶ Grammar Reference 9.2 p125

2 Look at the pictures. They tell a story. Match the sentences and pictures.

3 **a** They bought the painting for 1,400 francs.

6 **b** The man in the market was very upset. *—udiveny*

4 **c** They took the painting to an expert in Paris.

1 **d** Three friends went shopping in a market in France.

5 **e** The expert said the painting was worth 500 million francs.

2 **f** They saw a dirty, old painting for sale.

4 c

5 e

6 b

3 Read the story. Complete it with an irregular verb from exercise 1.

'We're millionaires!'

Florence Bayes in Paris

In August 1999 three friends, Jacques Proust, Guy Fadat, and François Leclerc, __were__ on holiday in the town of Laraque in France. On Sunday they _went_ shopping in the market and they _saw_ a dirty, old painting of the Virgin Mary. They _bought_ it for 1,400 francs and they _took_ it to Paris. In Paris, an expert said that the painting was by Leonardo da Vinci and it _was_ worth 500,000,000 francs. The man in Laraque market _said_ sold : 'I was happy to sell the painting but now I'm very upset. I don't want to think about it!'

---

nechum tomu over it,

sold

T 9.12 Listen and check.

Read the story to a partner.

4 Look at the pictures only and tell the story to a partner.

WORTH – CENA

upset – matený, znepokojený, udivený

EVERYDAY ENGLISH

When's your birthday?

สุขสันต์วันเกิด

HAPPY BIRTHDAY

happy

1   These are the months of the year. What is the correct order? Write them in the calendar.

MARCH   JUNE   OCTOBER   APRIL   FEBRUARY

NOVEMBER   MAY   JULY   SEPTEMBER   AUGUST

JANUARY		
1 2 3 4 5 6 7 8 9 10 11 12 13 14 15 16 17 18 19 20 21 22 23 24 25 26 27 28 29 30 31	1 2 3 4 5 6 7 8 9 10 11 12 13 14 15 16 17 18 19 20 21 22 23 24 25 26 27 28	1 2 3 4 5 6 7 8 9 10 11 12 13 14 15 16 17 18 19 20 21 22 23 24 25 26 27 28 29 30 31
1 2 3 4 5 6 7 8 9 10 11 12 13 14 15 16 17 18 19 20 21 22 23 24 25 26 27 28 29 30	1 2 3 4 5 6 7 8 9 10 11 12 13 14 15 16 17 18 19 20 21 22 23 24 25 26 27 28 29 30 31	1 2 3 4 5 6 7 8 9 10 11 12 13 14 15 16 17 18 19 20 21 22 23 24 25 26 27 28 29 30
1 2 3 4 5 6 7 8 9 10 11 12 13 14 15 16 17 18 19 20 21 22 23 24 25 26 27 28 29 30 31	1 2 3 4 5 6 7 8 9 10 11 12 13 14 15 16 17 18 19 20 21 22 23 24 25 26 27 28 29 30 31	1 2 3 4 5 6 7 8 9 10 11 12 13 14 15 16 17 18 19 20 21 22 23 24 25 26 27 28 29 30
		DECEMBER
1 2 3 4 5 6 7 8 9 10 11 12 13 14 15 16 17 18 19 20 21 22 23 24 25 26 27 28 29 30 31	1 2 3 4 5 6 7 8 9 10 11 12 13 14 15 16 17 18 19 20 21 22 23 24 25 26 27 28 29 30	1 2 3 4 5 6 7 8 9 10 11 12 13 14 15 16 17 18 19 20 21 22 23 24 25 26 27 28 29 30 31

T 9.13   Listen and check. Say the months round the class.

2   Which month is your birthday? Tell the class.

My birthday's in September.   *So is my birthday!*

How many birthdays are in each month? Which month has the most?

3   **T 9.14**   Listen and repeat the numbers.

first (1st)   second (2nd)   third (3rd)

fourth (4th)   fifth (5th)

sixth (6th)   seventh (7th)

eighth (8th)   ninth (9th)

tenth (10th)   eleventh (11th)

twelfth (12th)   thirteenth (13th)

fourteenth (14th)   fifteenth (15th)

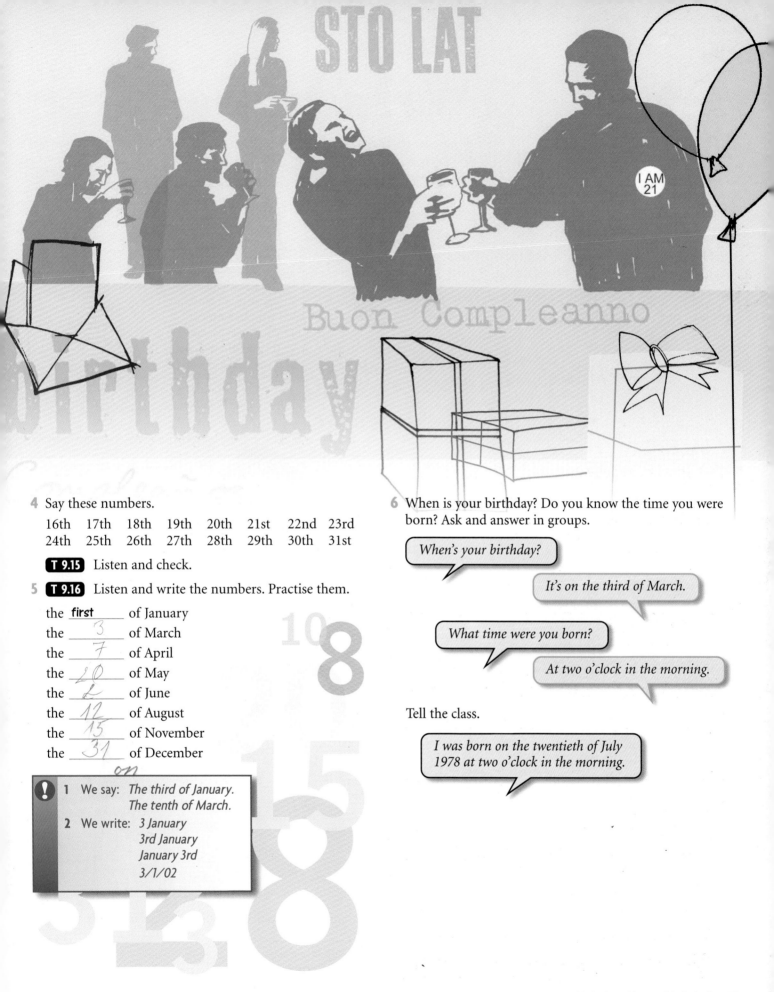

4 Say these numbers.

16th	17th	18th	19th	20th	21st	22nd	23rd
24th	25th	26th	27th	28th	29th	30th	31st

T 9.15 Listen and check.

5 **T 9.16** Listen and write the numbers. Practise them.

the **first** of January
the 3 of March
the 7 of April
the 20 of May
the 2 of June
the 12 of August
the 15 of November
the 31 of December

> **!** 1 We say: *The third of January.*
> *The tenth of March.*
>
> 2 We write: *3 January*
> *3rd January*
> *January 3rd*
> *3/1/02*

6 When is your birthday? Do you know the time you were born? Ask and answer in groups.

> *When's your birthday?*

> *It's on the third of March.*

> *What time were you born?*

> *At two o'clock in the morning.*

Tell the class.

> *I was born on the twentieth of July 1978 at two o'clock in the morning.*

10 We had a good time!

STARTER

1 What day is it today? What day was it yesterday? What's the date today? What date was it yesterday?

2 Match a line in **A** with a time expression in **B**.
   T 10.1 Listen, check, and repeat.

A	B
1 We're at school	now.
2 You were at home	yesterday.
3 I went to Australia	in 1997.
4 She lives in London	
5 They bought their house	
6 It was cold and wet	

YESTERDAY

Past Simple – regular and irregular

1 **T 10.2** Read the sentences and listen to Betsy. Tick (✓) the things she did yesterday.

2 Tell the class what she did.

> *Yesterday she got up late and she had a big …. Then she …*

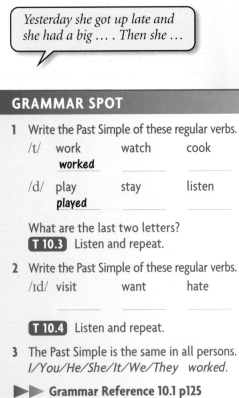

Yesterday she . . .
- ✓ got up late
- ✓ had a big breakfast
- ☐ played tennis
- ☐ went to work/school
- ✓ went shopping
- ☐ stayed at home
- ✓ bought a newspaper
- ✓ listened to music
- ☐ saw some friends
- ✓ watched TV
- ☐ worked at a computer
- ✓ cooked a meal
- ✓ went to bed early

GRAMMAR SPOT

1 Write the Past Simple of these regular verbs.

/t/	work	watch	cook
	worked		

/d/	play	stay	listen
	played		

What are the last two letters?
T 10.3 Listen and repeat.

2 Write the Past Simple of these regular verbs.

/ɪd/	visit	want	hate

T 10.4 Listen and repeat.

3 The Past Simple is the same in all persons.
I/You/He/She/It/We/They worked.

▶▶ **Grammar Reference 10.1 p125**

3 Underline the things in the list that you did yesterday. Talk to a partner.

> *Yesterday I got up late and went …*

Questions and negatives

4 **T 10.5** It's Monday morning. Listen to Betsy and Dan. Complete their conversation.

B Hi, Dan. Did you have a good weekend?
D Yes, I did, thanks.
B What did you do yesterday? _get_ ✓
D Well, yesterday morning I got up early and I _PLAYED_ tennis with some friends.
B You _GOT_ _UP_ early on Sunday!
D I know, I know. I don't usually get up early on Sunday.
B Did you go out yesterday afternoon?
D No, I didn't. I just _STAYED_ at home. I _watched_ the football on TV.
B Ugh, football! What did you do yesterday evening?
D Oh, I didn't do much. I _WORKED_ a bit at my computer. I didn't go to bed late. About 11.00. _eleven_

5 Complete the questions and answers from the conversation.
1 **B** _Did_ you _have_ a good weekend?
   D Yes, I did.
2 **B** What _did_ you _do_ yesterday?
   D I played tennis.
3 **B** _Did_ you _go_ out yesterday afternoon?
   D No, I didn't.
4 **B** What _did_ you _do_ yesterday evening?
   D I _didn't_ do much. I _didn't_ go to bed late.

T 10.6 Listen and check. Practise the questions and answers with a partner.

6 Look at the list in exercise 1 on p72. Ask and answer questions about Dan's weekend.

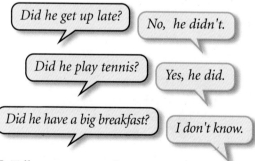

Did he get up late? *No, he didn't.*
Did he play tennis? *Yes, he did.*
Did he have a big breakfast? *I don't know.*

7 Talk to a partner about you. What *didn't* you do last weekend?

I didn't get up early.
I didn't play tennis.

PRACTICE

Did you have a good weekend?

1 Put a tick (✓) next to the things you did last weekend.

LAST WEEKEND			
Did you . . . ?	**You**	**Teacher**	**Partner**
go to the cinema	✓	✓	☐
go shopping	✓	✓	✓
have a meal in a restaurant	☐	✓	☐
see your friends	✓	✓	✓
play football	☐	☐	☐
go to a party	✓	☐	✓
do a lot of homework	✓	✓	✓
do a lot of housework	✓	✓	✓

2 Ask your teacher the questions. Put a (✓) next to the things she/he did.

> *Did you go to the cinema?*

> *Yes, I did./No, I didn't.*

3 Ask a partner the questions. Put a (✓) next to the things she/he did.

Tell the class about you and your partner.

> *Maria went to the cinema but I didn't. I went shopping.*

4 Make more questions with *did*.

1 What/see?   **What did you see?** *la netre*
2 What/buy? *shopping*
3 What/have? *restaurant*
4 Who/see? *saw my friends*
5 Where/play? *Played football*
6 What time/leave?
7 How much homework/do?
8 How much housework/do? *How much housework did you do*

T 10.8 Listen and check. What does the man say before the questions?

5 **T 10.9** Listen to the conversations. Practise them with a partner.

A Did you go to the cinema last weekend?
B Yes, I did.
A What did you see?
B I saw *The Boy from Bangkok*.
A Was it good?
B Yes, it was.

A Did you have a meal in a restaurant?
B Yes, we did.
A What did you have?
B We had steak and chips.
A Was it good?
B No, it wasn't. It was horrible!

Make similar conversations with your partner. Use the activities in exercise 1 and the questions in exercise 4.

6 Complete the short answers with *do/don't*, *does/doesn't*, or *did/didn't*.

1 Do you work in New York?   No, I **don't** .
2 Did she like the film ?   Yes, she **did** .
3 Does he watch TV every evening?   Yes, he *does* .
4 Did you go out yesterday evening?   No, we *didn't* .
5 Did he go to the party?   Yes, he *did* .
6 Do you buy a newspaper every morning?   Yes, I *do* .
7 Does she usually go to bed late?   No, she *doesn't* .
8 Did they have a good time?   No, they *didn't* .

T 10.10 Listen and check. Practise the questions and answers with a partner.

Check it

7 Tick (✓) the correct sentence.

1 ☑ She bought an expensive car.
   ☐ She buyed an expensive car.
2 ☐ Did they went shopping yesterday?
   ☑ Did they go shopping yesterday?
3 ☐ What did you go last weekend?
   ☑ Where did you go last weekend?
4 ☑ We didn't see our friends.
   ☐ We no saw our friends.
5 ☐ Did you like the film? Yes, I liked.
   ☑ Did you like the film? Yes, I did.
6 ☑ I played tennis yesterday.
   ☐ I play tennis yesterday.

VOCABULARY AND SPEAKING
Sports and leisure

be at leisure - mat volno
volnycas
lke

1 What are the activities in the photos?

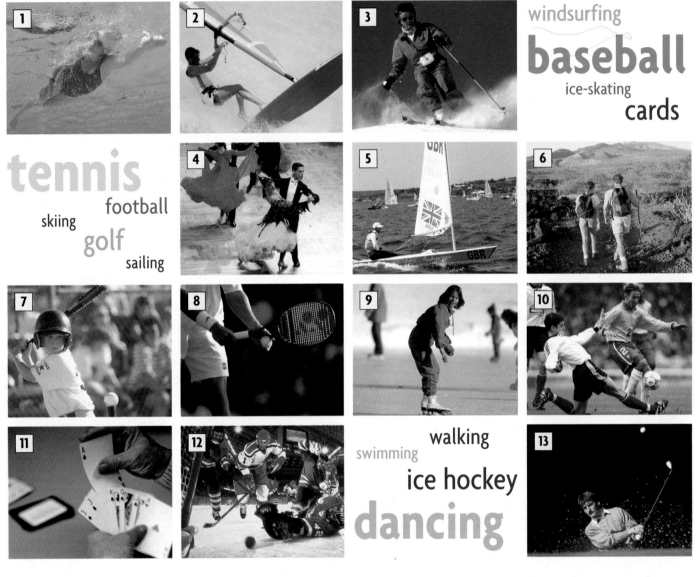

windsurfing

baseball

ice-skating

cards

tennis

skiing

football

golf

sailing

walking

swimming

ice hockey

dancing

2 Write the activities in the correct column.

play	go + -ing
tennis	skiing
baseball	swimming
football	windsurfing
cards	dancing
ice-hockey	sailing
golf	walking
	ice-skating

3 Ask and answer questions about the activities with a partner.

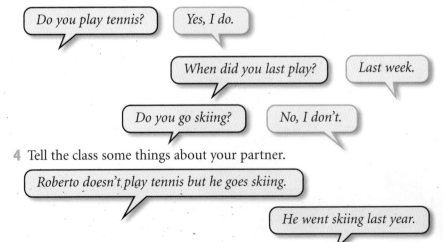

Do you play tennis?

Yes, I do.

When did you last play?

Last week.

Do you go skiing?

No, I don't.

4 Tell the class some things about your partner.

Roberto doesn't play tennis but he goes skiing.

He went skiing last year.

1 Say the months of the year. What are the four seasons?
When do you usually go on holiday?

> *We usually go on holiday in …*

2 **T 10.11** Listen to Colin and Fran talking about holidays.
<u>Underline</u> what they say.

A

They usually …
go in <u>summer</u> / spring.
go to France / <u>Spain.</u>
stay in a *hotel* / house.
eat in *the <u>hotel</u> / restaurants.*
go <u>swimming</u> / sailing.
play *tennis* / <u>golf.</u>
have / don't have a good time.

B

Last year they …
went in autumn / <u>winter.</u>
went to <u>Switzerland</u> / the US.
stayed in a *hotel* / chalet.
cooked their own meals / ate in restaurants.
went *skiing* / ice-skating / walking.
played *cards* / ice hockey.
had / didn't have a good time.

3 Ask and answer questions with a partner
about Colin and Fran's holidays.

- When / go?
- Where / go?
- Where / stay?
- Where / eat?
- What / do?
- … have a good time?

> *When do they usually go on holiday?*

> *In summer.*

> *When did they go last year?*

> *They went in winter.*

WRITING
My last holiday

1 Complete the sentences about Colin and Fran's last holiday. Use a negative, then a positive in the Past Simple.

1 Last year Colin and Fran __didn't go__ on holiday in summer.
They __went__ in winter.
2 They _didn't___ __go___ to Spain.
They _went___ to Switzerland.
3 They _didn't___ __go___ in a hotel.
They _stayed___ in a chalet. chata x žla
4 They _didn't___ __go___ in restaurants.
They _went to___ their own meals.
5 They _didn't___ __go___ swimming.
They _went___ skiing.

T 10.12 Listen and check.

2 Write about your last holiday.

My Last Holiday
Last ...
I went on holiday with ...
We went to ...
We stayed in ...
Every day we ...
We (sometimes/usually) ...
The weather was ...
We had/didn't have ...

Read it to the class.

Filling in forms

1 Jennifer Cottrell wants to join a sports centre. Look at her application form.

Olympic SPORTS CENTRE
APPLICATION FORM

Mr/Mrs/(Miss)/Ms *(please circle)*

Full name	Jennifer Alice Cottrell
Address	16, Latimer Road,
	Chesham,
	Buckinghamshire.
Postcode	HP7 1UV
Date of birth	17 3 1982
Telephone number	01494 765329
Nationality	Canadian
Signature	J A Cottrell
Date	4th February 2002

What sports are you interested in? *(please tick)*

swimming	✓
golf	
athletics	
tennis	
squash	
fitness training	✓

Do not write here

Type of card	
	HHSC/TSC/BSC/DAT
Data input date	

2 Fill in the same form for you.

Olympic SPORTS CENTRE
APPLICATION FORM

Mr/Mrs/Miss/Ms *(please circle)*

Full name	Nadzuja Halina Symanowicx
Address	Elblaska 16A/18
	Kranievo
	Wariminsko-Mazurskie
Postcode	14-500
Date of birth	15 02 1954
Telephone number	0048 55 6445025
Nationality	Polish
Signature	
Date	

What sports are you interested in? *(please tick)*

swimming	✓
golf	
athletics	✓
tennis	✓
squash	✓
fitness training	✓

Do not write here

Type of card	
	HHSC/TSC/BSC/DAT
Data input date	

3 Work in groups. Look at your application forms. Who is interested in what?

> Georges and I are both interested in athletics.

> Maria is interested in fitness training, but I'm not.

11 We can do it!

STARTER

1 Do you have a computer?
Do you use it for . . .
- homework?
- emails?
- shopping?
- computer games?
- the Internet?

2 Talk to a partner. Tell the class.

> I don't have a computer at home but I use the computer at work.

> I have a computer. I use it for shopping and I play computer games.

WHAT CAN THEY DO?
can/can't

1 Match the words and photos.

farmer	athlete	architect
interpreter	~~schoolboy~~	grandmother

2 Complete the sentences with *a* or *an* and a word from exercise 1.
  1 Josh is **a schoolboy**. He can use a computer.
  2 Sharon is _____. She can run fast.
  3 Lucy is _____. She can draw well.
  4 Ted is _____. He can speak French and German.
  5 Archie is _____. He can drive a tractor.
  6 Mabel is _____. She can make cakes.

  T 11.1 Listen and check. Practise the sentences.

3 Tell a partner what you can do from exercise 2.

> I can use a computer and I can make cakes.

1 Josh schoolboy
2 Sharon
4 Ted
3 Lucy

Questions and negatives

4 **T 11.2** Listen and repeat the questions and answers.

Can Josh use a computer? Yes, he can. *cen !!*

Can you use a computer? Yes, I can.

Can Lucy draw well? Yes, she can.

Can you draw well? No, I can't. I can't draw at all! *can't !!* *can not*

5 Ask and answer more questions with a partner. First ask about the people, then ask about your partner.

> Can Sharon run fast?

> Yes, she can.

> Can you run fast?

> No, I can't.

GRAMMAR SPOT

1 *Can/can't* have the same form for all persons.

I / You / He / She / It / We / They **can** draw.
can't *can't* = can not = negative

2 There is no *do/does* in the question.
I **can** speak French. **Can** you speak French?

3 **T 11.3** Listen and repeat the different pronunciations of *can*.

He can /kən/ speak Spanish. They can't /kɑːnt/ speak Spanish.
Can /kən/ you speak Spanish? Yes, I can /kæn/.

▶▶ **Grammar Reference 11.1 p126**

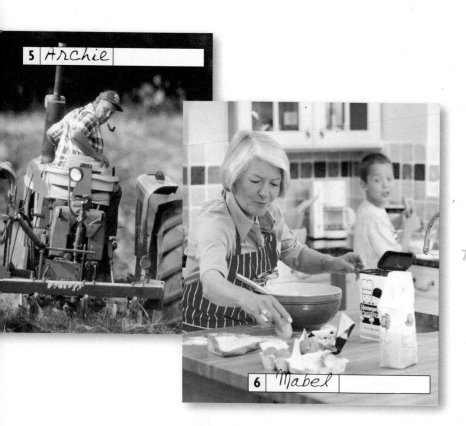

---

6 **T 11.4** Read and listen to Josh and Tessa. Complete the conversation.

T Can you use a computer, Josh?

J Yes, of course I **can**. All my friends **can**. I use a computer at school and at **home**.

T That's very good. What other things can you do?

J Well, I can **run** fast, very fast, and I can draw a bit. I can draw planes and **cars** very well but I can't drive a car of course. When I'm big I want to be a farmer and **drive** a tractor.

T And I know you can speak French.

J Yes, I can. I **can** speak French very well because my dad's French. We sometimes **speak** French at home.

T Can you speak any other languages?

J No, I **can't**. I can't speak German or Spanish, just French – and English of course! And I can cook! I can **make** cakes. My grandma makes lovely cakes and I sometimes help her. Yesterday we made a big chocolate cake.

Practise the conversation with a partner.

7 Answer the questions about Josh.

1 What can Josh do?
2 What can't Josh do?
3 Does he use a computer at school?
4 What does he want to be when he's big?
5 Why can he speak French well?
6 What did he do yesterday?

PRACTICE

Pronunciation

1 **T 11.5** Listen and <u>underline</u> what you hear, *can* or *can't*.

1 I <u>can</u> / *can't* use a computer.
2 She *can* / *can't* speak German.
3 He *can* / *can't* speak English very well.
4 Why *can* / *can't* you come to my party?
5 We *can* / *can't* understand our teacher.
6 They *can* / *can't* read music.
7 *Can* / *Can't* we have an ice-cream?
8 *Can* / *Can't* cats swim?

Listen again and repeat.

Can you or can't you?

2 **T 11.6** Listen to Tito. Tick (✓) the things he can do.

Can . . . ?	Tito	You	T	S
speak Spanish	✓			
speak French				
speak English very well				
drive a car				
ride a horse				
ski				
cook				
play the piano				
play the guitar				

Listen again and check.

3 Complete the chart about you. Then ask and answer the questions with the teacher and another student.

Can you speak Spanish?

No, I can't. Can you?

I can understand it but I can't speak it.

4 Compare yourself with the teacher and other students.

Isabel and I can speak French. She can speak Spanish too, but I can't.

82   Unit 11 · We can do it!

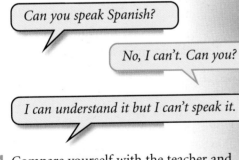

Requests and offers

5 Use the words to write questions with *Can*.

me **tell** time you the please

1 Can <u>you tell me the time, please</u> ?

speak you more slowly please

2 Can *yo speak more slowly?please*

come to my you party

3 Can *you come to my party?*

help I you

4 Can *I help you* ?

have cold I drink please a

5 Can *I have a cold drink? please*

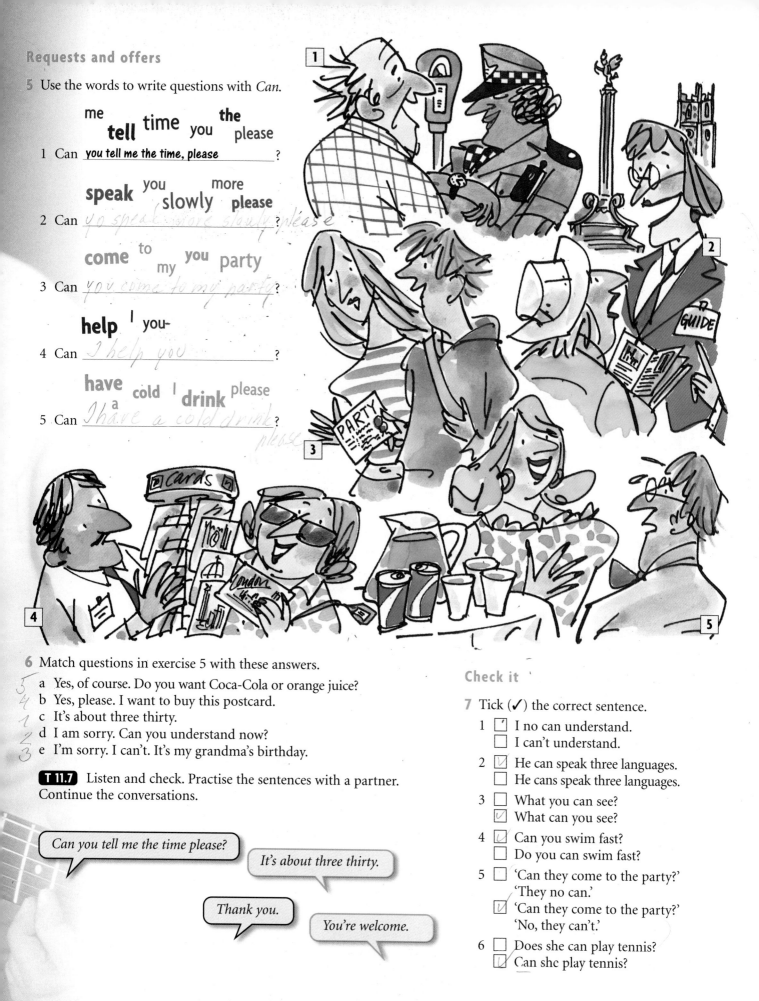

6 Match questions in exercise 5 with these answers.

5 a Yes, of course. Do you want Coca-Cola or orange juice?
4 b Yes, please. I want to buy this postcard.
1 c It's about three thirty.
2 d I am sorry. Can you understand now?
3 e I'm sorry. I can't. It's my grandma's birthday.

T 11.7 Listen and check. Practise the sentences with a partner. Continue the conversations.

Can you tell me the time please?

It's about three thirty.

Thank you.

You're welcome.

Check it

7 Tick (✔) the correct sentence.

1 ☑ I no can understand.
  ☐ I can't understand.

2 ☑ He can speak three languages.
  ☐ He cans speak three languages.

3 ☐ What you can see?
  ☑ What can you see?

4 ☑ Can you swim fast?
  ☐ Do you can swim fast?

5 ☐ 'Can they come to the party?'
    'They no can.'
  ☑ 'Can they come to the party?'
    'No, they can't.'

6 ☐ Does she can play tennis?
  ☑ Can she play tennis?

READING AND LISTENING
The things you can do on the Internet!

1 Match the verbs and nouns.

Verbs	Nouns
listen to	a hotel
watch	**a CD**
play	a magazine
read	a video
chat to	a friend
book	chess

2 Where do you find these addresses?
What does 'www' mean?

www.**shopping**.co.uk

www.**bbc**.co.uk

www.*chatshop*.com

www.weatherpage.vancouver.bc.ca

3 What do you know about the Internet?
Discuss these questions.

- When did the Internet start?
- Why did it start?
- What can you do on the Internet?

> *You can get a weather forecast.*

4 **T 11.8** Read and listen to the text
about the Internet. Answer the questions
in exercise 3.

5 Are the sentences true (✓) or false (✗)?
Correct the false (✗) sentences.

1 The Internet started in the 1980s.
2 Telephone companies started it.
3 It started in America.
4 There is an international computer
   language.

6 'The list is endless!'

Work in groups. Do you know any good
websites? Tell the class.

The Internet

Its history

The Internet started in the 1960s.
The United States Department of
Defense started it because they
wanted a computer network to help
the American military. In the 1970s
scientists worked on it. Then in the
1980s telephone companies made
it possible to communicate on
the computer network in many
more countries. An international
computer language was born,
and the Net went worldwide.

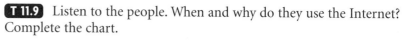

7 **T 11.9** Listen to the people. When and why do they use the Internet? Complete the chart.

	When?	Why?
Fleur	every day	help with homework
Anya		
Tito		
Henry		
Tommy		
Iris		

T 11.9 Listen again and check.

What can it do?

You can use the Internet for many things. You can buy a car or a house; you can book a holiday; you can watch a video; you can read an Australian newspaper or a Japanese magazine; you can buy books and CDs from North and South America; you can play chess with a partner in Moscow; or you can just chat to people from all over the world. The list is endless!

EVERYDAY ENGLISH

What's the problem?

1 Here are some problems. Check that you understand them.

'The TV's broken.'

'This ticket machine doesn't work.'

'I don't understand this word.'

'I'm lost.'

2 Complete the conversations with the problems from exercise 1.

1 A Come on! It's time to go to the airport.

   B But _____.

   A You put it in your bag.

   B Did I? Oh, yes. Here it is! Phew!

2 A Excuse me!

   B Yes?

   A _____.
I put in two pounds, but I didn't get a ticket.

   B Did you push this button?

   A Oh! No, I didn't.

   B Ah, well. Here you are.

   A Thank you very much.

3 A Excuse me.

   B Yes?

   A Can you help me?

   _____.

   B Where do you want to go?

   A To the railway station.

   B Go straight on. About two hundred metres. It's on your left.

T 11.10 Listen and check.

3 Practise the conversations with a partner. Learn two conversations and act them to the class.

'I can't find my passport.'

'I forgot your birthday.'

4 **A** _____.
  B Check it in your dictionary.
  A My dictionary's at home. Can
     I borrow yours?
  B OK. No problem. Here you are.

5 **A** Oh no!
  B What's the matter?
  A _____.
  B Good! Perhaps we can talk this
     evening.
  A But I want to watch a film.
  B Go to the cinema, then.

6 **A** I'm really sorry.
  _____
  B It doesn't matter.
  A It was on the tenth, wasn't it?
  B Yes, it was.
  A Well, here are some flowers.
  B Oh, thank you very much.
     They're beautiful.

12 Thank you very much!

want and *would like* · Food and drink · In a restaurant · Going shopping

1 Match the activities and the places.

A	B
buy stamps 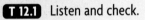	in a bank
buy a dictionary	in a music shop
buy a computer magazine	in a book shop
change money	in an Internet café
buy a CD	in a café
get a cup of coffee	in a post office
send an email	in a newsagent

2 Make sentences beginning *You can . . .*   **You can buy stamps in a post office.**

T 12.1 Listen and check.

A TRIP INTO TOWN
want and *would like*

1 Look at Enrique's shopping list.
What does he want?

> *He wants a stamp.*

> *He wants to change his money.*

a stamp for a
letter to Venezuela

change my money

Gary Alright's new CD

send an email to
Rosa in the US

a Spanish/English
dictionary

a PC Worldwide
computer magazine

2 **T 12.2** Read and listen to Enrique's conversations in town. Complete the sentences.

1 E Good morning. _I'd like_
a stamp for this letter to
Venezuela, please.
A That's 75p.
E Thank you.
A Here you are, and 25p
change.
E Thanks a lot. Bye.

2 E _I'd like_ a cup of
coffee, please.
B _Would you like_ black or
white?
E Black, please.
B All right. Here you are. One
pound twenty, please.

3 E Hello. _I'd like_ to buy
a Spanish / English dictionary.
C OK. _Would you like_ a big
dictionary or a minidictionary?
E Just a minidictionary, please.
C This one is £4.99.
E That's fine. Thank you very
much.

3 **T 12.3** Listen and repeat.

> *I'd like a stamp.*

> *I'd like a cup of coffee.*

> *Would you like black or white?*

> *I'd like to buy a dictionary.*

> *Would you like a big dictionary or a minidictionary?*

Work with a partner. Practise the conversations in exercise 2.

GRAMMAR SPOT

1 *I'd like* ... (*'d* = would) is more polite than *I want* ....
   I'd like a coffee, please.
   I'd like to buy a dictionary, please.
2 We offer things using *Would you like* ...?
   Would you like a cup of tea? No, thank you.
   Would you like to come to a party on Saturday? Yes, please.

▶▶ **Grammar Reference 12.1 p126**

---

4 **T 12.4** Listen to more conversations with
Enrique. Where is he? Write a number 1–5.

☐ a newsagent *he buy*
☐ an Internet café
☐ a music shop
☐ a bank
☐ a cinema

Look at the tapescript on p119. Practise
the conversations.

PRACTICE

What would you like?

1 Your friend is at your house. Make him/her feel at home!
Use the ideas.

- a drink
- a cup of coffee
- a sandwich
- some cake
- listen to music
- play cards
- watch a video
- play a computer game

> Would you like a drink?

> Yes, please./No thanks.

> What would you like?

> An orange juice, please.

> Would you like to listen to music?

> That's a good idea!

It's my birthday!

2 **T 12.5** Listen to these people. It's their birthday soon.
Complete the chart.

	What would she/he like?	What would she/he like to do in the evening?
Suzanne	in bed with newspaper evening	
Tom	computer a lot restaurant Italian wine	
Alice	PHONE WITH FRIEND GREAT TIME	

3 It's *your* birthday soon! Ask and answer the questions
with a partner.

> What would you like?

> I'd like a CD.

> I'd like a new car!

> What would you like to do on your birthday?

> I'd like to go out for a meal.

> I'd like to have a party.

Talking about you

4 Work with a partner. Ask and answer the questions.

- Do you like travelling?
- Where do you like going?
- Where would you like to go next?
- Would you like to live in another country?
- Would you like to live in the United States?
- Do you like learning English?
- Would you like to learn more languages?

Why?/Why not?

> *Do you like travelling?*

> *Yes, I do./No, I don't.*

> *Where would you like to go next?*

> *I'd like to go to Turkey.*

GRAMMAR SPOT

1 We use *like* to talk about always.

I **like** coffee.   I **don't like** tea.   I **like** swimming.

2 We use *'d like* to talk about now or a time in the future.

I**'d like** a coffee please.   I**'d like** to go to Mexico next year.

▶▶ **Grammar Reference 12.2 p126**

Listening and pronunciation

5 **T 12.6** Tick (✓) the sentence you hear.

1 ☐ Would you like a Coke?
  ☐ Do you like Coke?

2 ☐ I like orange juice.
  ☐ I'd like an orange juice.

3 ☐ We like going for walks.
  ☐ We'd like to go for a walk.

4 ☐ What do you like doing at the weekend?
  ☐ What would you like to do this weekend?

5 ☐ We'd like a new car.
  ☐ We like our new car.

Check it

6 Tick (✓) the correct sentence.

1 ☐ I like to go home now, please.
  ☐ I'd like to go home now, please.

2 ☐ What would you like to do?
  ☐ What would you like do?

3 ☐ I like swimming.
  ☐ I'd like swimming.

4 ☐ You like a coffee?
  ☐ Would you like a coffee?

5 ☐ Do you like listen to music?
  ☐ Do you like listening to music?

VOCABULARY AND SPEAKING

In a restaurant

1 Match the food and photos. Write the words.

fish	cheese	salad	mineral water	soup
vegetables	chicken	fries	tomato	fruit

T 12.7 Listen and repeat.

1 cheese

2 fish

3 fruit

4 salad

5 vegetables

6 chicken

7 soup

8 tomato

9 fries

10 m. water

2 Complete the menu with the words.

beer   roast chicken

cheese   ~~tomato soup~~   apple pie and cream

mixed salad   mineral water

cheeseburger

Joe's DINER

To start
seafood cocktail
| tomato soup |

Burgers
hamburger, salad and fries
| _cheeseburger_ |, salad and fries

Sandwiches
ham
chicken
| _roast chicken_ |

Meat
steak and fries
| _MIXED SALAD_ | and salad

Side orders
fries
| _CHEESE_ |

Desserts
ice-cream
chocolate cake
| _APPLE PIE AND CREAM_ |

To drink
wine
orange juice
| _BEER_ |
| _MINERAL WATER_ |

3 **T 12.8** Listen to Renate and Paul ordering a meal in Joe's Diner. Who says these things? Write *W*, *R*, or *P*.

W = the waiter   R = Renate   P = Paul

- [P] Renate, what would you like to start?
- [ ] Can I have the tomato soup, please?
- [ ] And I'd like the seafood cocktail.
- [ ] Can I have the steak, please?
- [ ] How would you like it cooked?
- [ ] What would you like to drink?
- [ ] And we'd like a bottle of mineral water, too.
- [ ] Delicious, thank you.

4 Look at the tapescript on p119. Practise the conversation in groups of three.

5 Have more conversations in Joe's Diner. Use the menu.

READING

She only eats junk food

1 Look at the words.
What food is good for you?

2 What's your favourite food?
Tell the class.

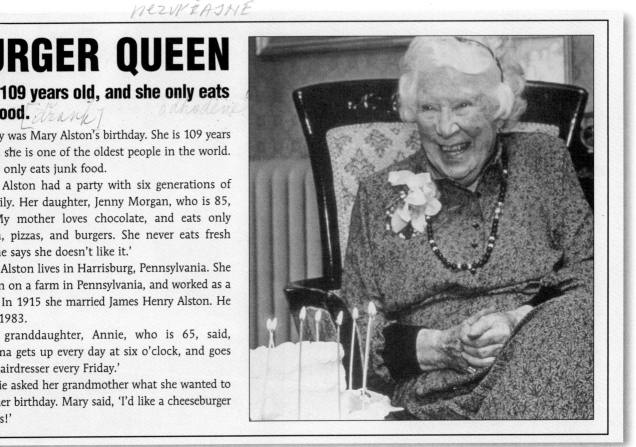

fruit · BURGERS · fish · vegetables · chocolate · pizza · fries

3 Read the newspaper article. What's unusual about Mary Alston?

nezvyčajné

BURGER QUEEN

She's 109 years old, and she only eats junk food. *[zrank]* *odhodene*

Yesterday was Mary Alston's birthday. She is 109 years old, and she is one of the oldest people in the world. And she only eats junk food.

Mrs Alston had a party with six generations of her family. Her daughter, Jenny Morgan, who is 85, said, 'My mother loves chocolate, and eats only popcorn, pizzas, and burgers. She never eats fresh food. She says she doesn't like it.'

Mrs Alston lives in Harrisburg, Pennsylvania. She was born on a farm in Pennsylvania, and worked as a teacher. In 1915 she married James Henry Alston. He died in 1983.

Her granddaughter, Annie, who is 65, said, 'Grandma gets up every day at six o'clock, and goes to the hairdresser every Friday.'

Annie asked her grandmother what she wanted to eat on her birthday. Mary said, 'I'd like a cheeseburger and fries!'

4 Match the questions and answers. Complete the sentences.

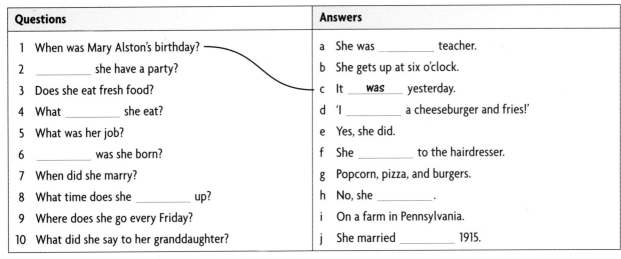

Questions	Answers
1 When was Mary Alston's birthday?	a She was _____ teacher.
2 _____ she have a party?	b She gets up at six o'clock.
3 Does she eat fresh food?	c It _____was_____ yesterday.
4 What _____ she eat?	d 'I _____ a cheeseburger and fries!'
5 What was her job?	e Yes, she did.
6 _____ was she born?	f She _____ to the hairdresser.
7 When did she marry?	g Popcorn, pizza, and burgers.
8 What time does she _____ up?	h No, she _____.
9 Where does she go every Friday?	i On a farm in Pennsylvania.
10 What did she say to her granddaughter?	j She married _____ 1915.

T 12.9 Listen and check. Practise the questions and answers with a partner.

EVERYDAY ENGLISH

Going shopping

1 **T 12.10** Listen to the conversations in different places. Use the words to complete the conversations.

In the street

1 **A** Excuse me! <u>Where can I buy a film</u> for my camera? | can film a Where I buy

   B In a chemist.

   A _____? | there a Is chemist here near

   B Yes, two hundred metres from here, _____. | bank the to next

In a clothes shop

2 **C** Can I help you?

   A _____. I'm just looking. | thanks No,

3 **A** Excuse me! _____ in a medium? | have shirt Do you this

   C No, I'm sorry. _____. | all we That's have

4 **A** _____ a pair of jeans, please. | try like to I'd on

   C Sure. _____? | are size What you

   A I think I'm a forty.

   C Fine. The changing rooms are over there.

At the market

5 **D** Yes, madam. _____? | like you would What

   A _____ potatoes, please. | kilo a like I'd of

   D Anything else?

   A _____, thanks. How much is that? | that's No, all

In a newsagent

6 **A** Excuse me! _____ newspapers? | Spanish sell Do you

   E _____, we don't. | sorry No, I'm

   A Where _____? | them buy can I

   E Try the railway station.

2 Work with a partner. Have similar conversations. You want these things.

Student A
- a birthday card
- this jumper (small / medium / large)
- apples
- pens

Student B
- a phone card
- this T-shirt (small / medium / large)
- tomatoes
- computer magazines

13 Here and now

Colours and clothes · Present Continuous · Questions and negatives · What's the matter?

STARTER

1 Look at the pictures of George and Sadie. Find the colours.

George

Sadie

black
white
red
blue
green
grey
yellow
brown

2 Complete the sentences with the colours.

1 George's jacket is **black**. Sadie's jacket is *red*.
2 His trousers are *grey*. Her trousers are *green*.
3 Her shirt is *yellow*. His shirt is *white*.
4 Her shoes are *blue*. His shoes are *brown*.

T 13.1 Listen and check. Practise the sentences.

3 What colours are your clothes today?

WORK AND HOLIDAYS
Present Continuous

1 Read about George's job. Complete the text with the verbs.

goes   has   ~~works~~   reads   enjoys   starts   leaves   wears

George _works_ in a bank. He _starts_ work at 9.00 and he _leaves_ work at 5.30. He always _wears_ a black jacket and grey trousers. He _has_ lunch at 1.00. He sometimes _goes_ to the park and _reads_ his newspaper. He _enjoys_ his job.

2 **T 13.2** Listen and read about George on holiday.

Now George is on holiday in Thailand with his wife. He's wearing a white T-shirt. His wife is reading a book. They're having lunch. 'We're having a great holiday,' says George.

3 **T 13.3** Listen and repeat.

He's wearing a T-shirt.   She's reading a book.
They're having lunch.   We're having a great holiday.

4 Make true sentences about George's holiday.

George		swimming.
His wife		reading the menu.
Four people	is	playing tennis.
Two people	are	enjoying our holiday.
We		having lunch.
They		wearing a blue T-shirt.

GRAMMAR SPOT

1 George **is wearing** a white T-shirt. He**'s having** lunch.

These sentences say what George is doing *now*. This is the Present Continuous tense.

2 We make the Present Continuous with *am/are/is* + verb + *-ing*.

3 Complete the sentences. Use the verbs.

I _am_ _studying_ English. (study)
You _are_ _wearing_ jeans. (wear)
She _is_ _reading_ a book. (read)
We _are_ _working_ in class. (work)
They _are_ _having_ lunch. (have)

▶▶ **Grammar Reference 13.1 p127**

PRACTICE

Speaking

1 Work with a partner. What are these people doing?

He's cooking.

silvet taking

T 13.4 Listen and check.   *endless*

2 Think of actions you can mime to your partner. Can your partner guess what you are doing?   *whadne*

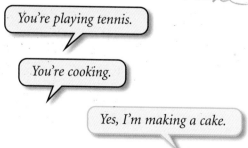

You're playing tennis.

You're cooking.

Yes, I'm making a cake.

I'M WORKING
Questions and negatives

1 **T 13.5** Read and listen to a radio interview with the model, Sadie.

Radio Milano 105.9FM
transcript

Parliamone 14.05 pm 05|02 [**I** – Interviewer, **S** – Sadie]

I What are you doing here in Milan, Sadie?
S I'm working. There is a big fashion show here.
I Are you staying in a hotel?
S No, I'm not. I'm staying with friends.
I Are you having a good time in Milan?
S Yes, I am. I'm enjoying it very much.
I Now Sadie, tell the listeners. What are you wearing now?
S I'm not wearing anything special! I'm just wearing jeans and a T-shirt.
I Thank you, Sadie. It was nice to talk to you.
S Thank you.

2 Ask and answer the questions with *she*.
   1 What ... doing in Milan?
   2 Where ... staying?
   3 ... having a good time?
   4 What ... wearing?

> *What's she doing in Milan?*

> *She's working.*

GRAMMAR SPOT

Present Continuous

1 **Questions**
   What are you wearing?
   Where's she staying?

2 **Negatives**
   I'm not staying in a hotel.
   He isn't working.
   We aren't having breakfast.

3 **Short answers**
   Are they having a good time? Yes, they are.
   Are you working? No, I'm not.

▶▶ **Grammar Reference 13.2 and 13.3 p127**

PRACTICE

Asking questions

1 Look at the answers. Write the questions. Use the verbs.

(read)
What are you reading?

A love story.

(watch)

The news.

(go)

To my bedroom.

T 13.6 Listen and check.

(wear / three jumpers)

Because I'm cold.

(eat)

Chocolate.

(make)

Five.

(talk to)

My girlfriend.

2 Write the questions.

1 you / wear / a new jumper ?
2 we / learn / Chinese?
3 we / sit / in our classroom? *yes we are*
4 you / wear / new shoes?
5 the teacher / wear / blue trousers?
6 it / rain? *it isn't*
7 all the students / speak / English?
8 you / learn / a lot of English?

Stand up. Ask and answer the questions.

Are you wearing a new jumper?

Yes, I am.

Are we learning Chinese?

No, we aren't. We're learning English.

Check it

3 Tick (✓) the correct sentence.

1 ☐ I'm wear a blue shirt today.
   ☑ I'm wearing a blue shirt today.
2 ☑ Where are you going?
   ☐ Where you going?
3 ☐ Peter no working this week.
   ☑ Peter isn't working this week.
4 ☐ That's Peter over there. He talks to the teacher.
   ☑ That's Peter over there. He's talking to the teacher.
5 ☑ Heidi is German. She comes from Berlin.
   ☐ Heidi is German. She's coming from Berlin. *now*

Who are you talking to

Today's different

1 What do you usually do on Saturday? On your birthday? On Christmas Day? On Sunday evening?

2 Read one of the texts. Match a photograph 1–4 with your text.

3 Answer the questions about your text.
   1 What does he/she usually do on this day?
   2 Why is today different?
   3 What is he/she doing?
   4 What happened this morning?
   5 What is he/she wearing?
   6 What are the people in the photographs doing?

4 Work in groups of four. Tell the others about your person. Use your answers in exercise 3.

A photo of me

Bring a photograph of you to class. Say …
- where you are.
- what you're doing.
- who you're with.
- what you're wearing.

Isabel

❝On Saturday mornings I usually get up late and do the housework. Then I meet some friends in town for lunch, and go shopping in the afternoon.❞

But this Saturday is different! This morning Isabel got up early because today she's getting married. She's in church with all her family and friends. She's wearing a white dress, and her husband is standing next to her.

Leo

❝On my birthday I sometimes go out with friends, or I go out to a restaurant with my family. My Mum usually makes me a birthday cake.❞

But this birthday is different! It's Leo's eighteenth birthday, so now he's an adult. This morning he got a lot of presents. Now he's having a big party with all his friends. They're dancing and drinking beer. Leo's wearing a blue jumper.

Mark

❝On Christmas Day we usually all go to my parents' house. We open our presents, then have a big lunch at about 2.00 in the afternoon.❞

But this Christmas is different! Mark and his wife are in Australia. They're visiting friends. This morning they went to church, and now they're having a barbecue next to the swimming pool. It's hot and they're wearing swimsuits.

Becca

'I usually hate Sunday evenings because I don't like Mondays. I do my homework and get ready for school.

But this Sunday evening is different! Becca's getting ready to go on a skiing holiday tomorrow. This morning she went to a friend's house, then she had lunch with her grandparents. Now she's packing her bags. She's trying on her ski clothes. She's enjoying this Sunday evening.

BECCA

VOCABULARY AND SPEAKING
Clothes

1 Match the clothes and the photos. Write the words.

a shirt	boots	a skirt	shorts	a jumper
shoes	sandals	trousers	a dress	a jacket
trainers	a coat	a hat	a tie	socks

T 13.7 Listen and repeat. Which two items of clothing are only for women?

2 Say what the people are wearing.

She's wearing a red and black skirt and a grey jumper.

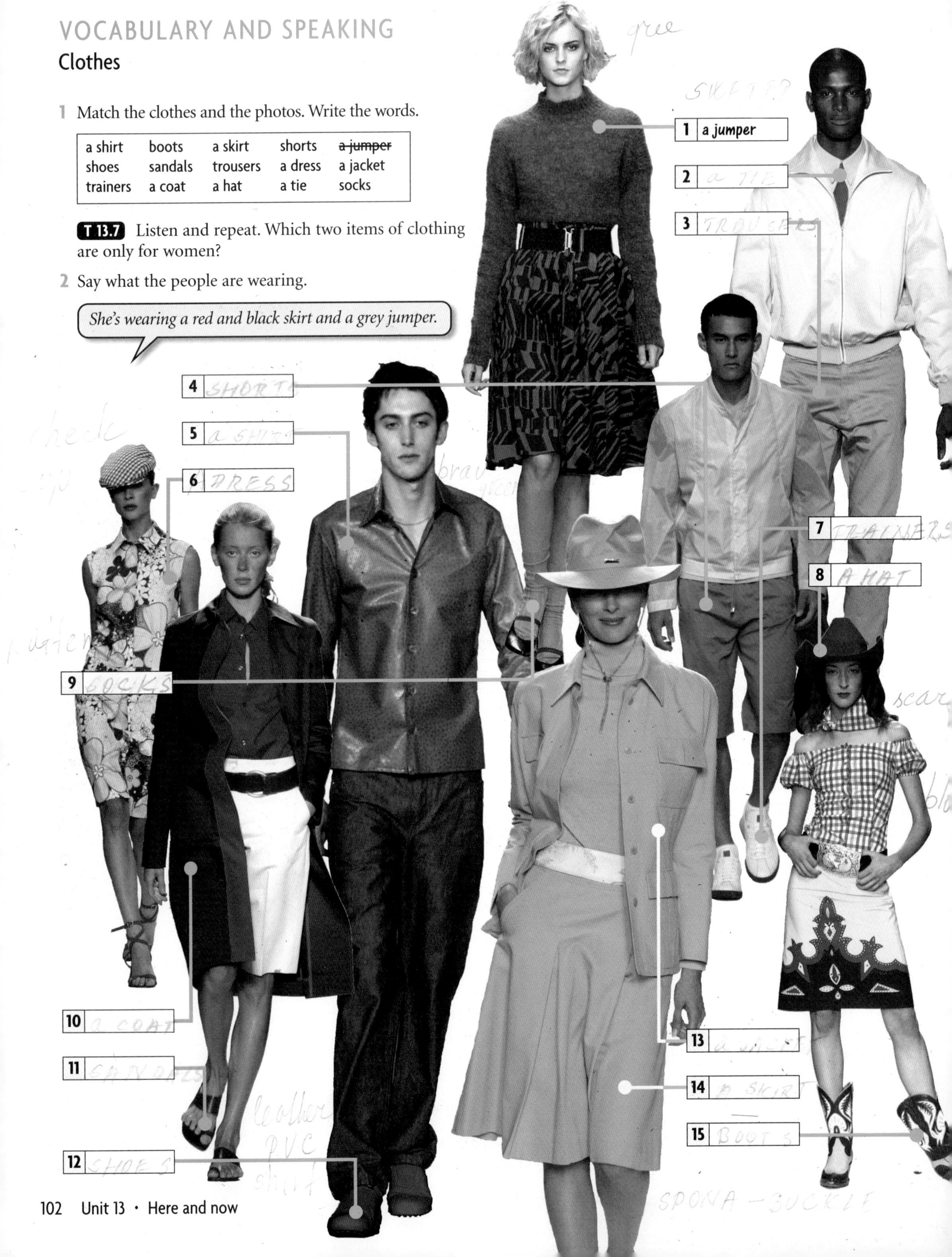

1 a jumper

2 *a TIE*

3 *TROUSERS*

4 *SHORTS*

5 *a SHIRT*

6 *DRESS*

7 *TRAINERS*

8 *A HAT*

9 *SOCKS*

10 *a COAT*

11 *SANDALS*

12 *SHOES*

13 *a JACKET*

14 *a SKIRT*

15 *BOOTS*

3 Stand back to back with another student. Ask questions to find out what he/she is wearing.

> *Are you wearing jeans?*

> *No, I'm not.*

> *Are you wearing trousers?*

> *Yes, I am.*

> *Are they black?*

> *Yes, they are.*

4 Practise with a partner. Ask and answer the questions.

- What are your favourite colours?
- What are your favourite clothes?
- What do you wear during the week?
- What about at the weekend?

5 **T 13.8** Listen and complete the sentences with these words.

eyes short brown fair

1 She has long, _brown_ hair.
2 He has _short_, black hair.
3 She has blue _eyes_.
4 He has _fair_ eyes.

6 Describe a person in the room, but don't say who it is. Can the other students guess who it is?

> *She has brown hair and brown eyes. She's wearing … , and she's sitting …*

EVERYDAY ENGLISH

What's the matter?

1 What's the matter with the people? Complete the sentences with these words.

tired hungry thirsty ~~cold~~ hot bored

1 She's **cold**.

2 He's _hungry_

3 They're _tired_

4 He's _thirsty_

5 They're _hot_

6 She's _bored_
[bed]

T 13.9 Listen and repeat.

2 **T 13.10** Listen to the conversation. Practise with a partner.

A What's the matter?
B I'm tired and thirsty.
A Why don't you have a cup of tea?
B That's a good idea.

3 Have similar conversations. Use the words from exercise 1 and these ideas.

- go to bed early
- have a cold drink
- sit down and relax
- put on a jumper
- go for a swim
- go to the cinema
- have a sandwich
- watch a video
- have a shower

14 It's time to go!

Present Continuous for future · Question word revision · Transport and travel · Going sightseeing

STARTER

1 What year is it? What year is it next year?
What month is it? What month is it next month?
What day is it today? What day is it tomorrow?

2 Say the months of the year and the days of the week round the class.

HOLIDAY PLANS

Present Continuous for future

1 **T 14.1** Listen to Ellie and read her diary for next week. Why is she excited?

APRIL

6 Monday
collect tickets from the travel agent

7 Tuesday
meet Ed and Lucy after work
go shopping

8 Wednesday
11.00 a.m. see the doctor
have lunch with mum

9 Thursday
leave work early
pack bags

10 Friday
6.30 a.m. go by taxi to the airport
meet Ed and Lucy
9.30 a.m. fly to Mexico

11 Saturday

12 Sunday

APRIL
M T W T F S S
    1 2 3 4 5
6 7 8 9 10 11 12
13 14 15 16 17 18 19
20 21 22 23 24 25 26
27 28 29 30

2 Complete the sentences about Ellie.

1 On Monday she's collecting her ___tickets___ from the travel agent.

2 On Tuesday she's meeting Ed and Lucy after _____ and they're going _____.

3 On Wednesday she's seeing the _____ at 11 o'clock, then she's _____ lunch with her mother.

4 On Thursday she's _____ work early and she's _____ her bags.

5 On Friday at 6.30 in the morning she's going by _____ to the airport and she's _____ Ed and Lucy there. At 9.30 they're _____ to Mexico.

GRAMMAR SPOT

1 The Present Continuous can express future plans.
I'm going to Mexico <u>next week</u>.
She's seeing the doctor on Wednesday.
We're leaving next Friday.

2 We often say when (this afternoon, tomorrow, on Saturday, . . .) with the Present Continuous. Underline the time expressions in Grammar Spot 1.

▶▶ **Grammar Reference 14.1 p127**

Questions

3 **T 14.2** Listen and repeat the question and answer.

What's she doing on Monday?
She's collecting her tickets.

Ask and answer more questions about Ellie's week. Work with a partner.

> What's she doing on Tuesday?
> She's …

4 Write your diary for the next four days. Ask and answer questions with a partner.

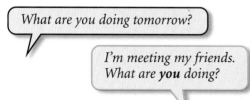

> What are you doing tomorrow?
> I'm meeting my friends. What are **you** doing?

5 Look at the picture. It's Monday morning. Ellie's at work. What is she doing? Complete the conversation with the question words.

| ~~what~~ | when | where | how | who | why |

A ___What___ are you doing?
E I'm reading about Mexico.
A _____?
E Because I'm going there on holiday soon.
A Oh lovely! _____ are you leaving?
E We're leaving next Friday.
A _____ are you going with?
E My friends Ed and Lucy.
A _____ are you travelling?
E We're travelling by plane to Mexico City, then by bus and train around the country.
A _____ are you staying?
E We're staying in small hotels and hostels.
A You're so lucky! Have a good time!
E Thanks very much.

T 14.3 Listen and check. Practise with a partner.

GRAMMAR SPOT

1 Make the question form with *When* and *I / you / he / she / we / they*.
When am I leaving?   When are you leaving?   When is he . . . ?

2 The Present Continuous can express present and future.
Which sentence is about now? Which sentence is about the future?
I'm reading about Mexico.   I'm leaving next Friday.

▶▶ **Grammar Reference 14.1 p127**

PRACTICE

Listening and speaking

1 Look at the chart about Marco's holiday plans. Write the questions.

   Where is he going?
   Why is he going there?
   When ... ?

   T 14.4 Listen and check the questions. Complete the chart about Marco's holiday plans.

2 Ask and answer the questions about Marco with a partner.

Marco

Where / go?	Banff, Canada
Why / go?	to go skiing
When / leave?	
How / travel?	
Where / stay?	Banff Springs Hotel
How long / stay?	

Where's he going?

He's going to Banff, in Canada.

3 Look at the pictures. Where are the people going on holiday, do you think?

Rachel + Lara

Didier

Work with a partner.

Student A Look at p139. Read about Rachel and Lara's holiday plans.

Student B Look at p140. Read about Didier's holiday plans.

Ask and answer the questions to complete your chart.

4 Ask and answer the questions about you.

> *Where are you going for your next holiday?*

> *To England.*

> *Why are you going there?*

> *Because I want to practise my English.*

Tell the class about your partner.

> *Juan is going to England because he wants to practise his English. He's …*

5 Read the sentences about yesterday and ask a question about tomorrow.

Yesterday	Tomorrow
1 I got up early.	*Are you getting up early tomorrow?*
2 I went swimming.	*Are you going . . . ?*
3 I walked to work.	
4 I had lunch in my office.	
5 I left work late.	
6 I met a friend.	
7 We had dinner in a restaurant.	

T 14.5 Listen, check, and repeat. Practise the intonation in the questions.

6 Write what you did yesterday. Tell a partner. Ask and answer questions about tomorrow.

> *I went to my English class.*

> *Are you going to your English class tomorrow?*

> *No, I'm not. I'm …*

Check it

7 Tick (✔)the correct sentence.

1 ☑ I'm leaving tomorrow.
 ☐ I leaving tomorrow.
2 ☐ We go to the cinema this evening.
 ☑ We're going to the cinema this evening.
3 ☐ Where they go on holiday?
 ☑ Where are they going on holiday?
4 ☐ Where are you doing on Saturday evening?
 ☑ What are you doing on Saturday evening?
5 ☐ What do you do tomorrow?
 ☑ What are you doing tomorrow?

READING

An amazing journey

1 Can you drive? Do you like driving? What is your favourite car?

2 Look at the photograph and the map. Who are the people? How old is their car? What kind of car is it? Where did their journey start and finish?

3 Read about John Pollard's car. Are the sentences true (✔) or false (✗)? Correct the false (✗) sentences.

1 John Pollard bought a VW. ✗   **He didn't buy a VW. He bought a Mini.**

2 He bought it in 1964. ✔

3 He bought the Mini when he was a student.

4 He paid £250,000 for it.

5 He went to Russia three times in his old Mini.

6 He married, then he went to Australia.

7 John and his wife stayed in Australia because they had no money.

8 They're buying a new Mini soon.

9 They're returning to Australia by ship.

10 The Mini isn't staying in England.

4 Complete the interview with John.

I   This is an amazing car, John. When did you buy it?

JP _I 1964_, when I was a student.

I   And how much did it cost?

JP _Just £505_

I   Why did you buy it?

JP Because I _wanted_ to travel. In 1966 _I drove to_ Moscow, Finland, and the Arctic Circle.

I   Does your wife like the Mini?

JP Oh, yes. She loves it. We _married_ in 1967 and we _drove the Mini to_ Australia via India. We stayed in Australia _30_ years.

I   When did you come back to England?

JP _Last month_

I   Are you going back to Australia?

JP Yes, we are. We _are returning_ next month.

I   Are you leaving the Mini in England?

JP No we aren't. The Mini _travels_ by ship.

T 14.6   Listen and check. Practise the conversation in pairs.

To Aust

IN 1964 John Pollard bought a new car. It was a Mini, and it cost just £505. 250,000 miles later he is still driving it. Mr Pollard, 59, said: 'I bought the car when I was a student. I wanted to travel. In 1966 I drove to

JOHN AND CARYS POLLARD with their 1964 Mini car. 250,000 miles and still going strong.

Moscow, Finland, and the Arctic Circle. I married in 1967 and then my wife and I drove the Mini to Australia via India. I found a job in Sydney, and we stayed in Australia for 30 years. We used the Mini all the time. Last month we came back to England to visit our families and of course, we came in the Mini. We drove via Kuala Lumpur, Bangkok, Tibet and China, Mongolia, and Russia.'

Mr and Mrs Pollard love their old Mini and don't want to sell it and buy a new one. 'Next month we're returning to Australia but we are not driving, we are travelling by plane. The Mini is travelling by ship. We decided to give it a rest for the return journey because it is very old and tired.'

VOCABULARY AND SPEAKING

Transport and travel

1 Match the transport and pictures.

> bicycle   ship   the Underground   motorbike

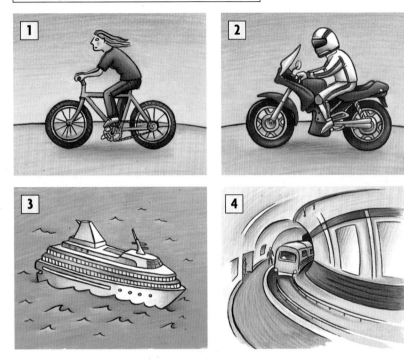

2 Work with a partner. How many other forms of transport do you know?

3 Match a verb in **A** with words in **B**.

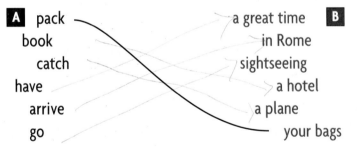

A	B
pack	a great time
book	in Rome
catch	sightseeing
have	a hotel
arrive	a plane
go	your bags

4 Put the sentences in the correct order.

- ☐ 1 We wanted to have a holiday in Rome.
- ☐ 6 We caught the plane.
- ☐ We went to the airport.
- ☐ 2 We booked the hotel and the flight.
- ☐ We packed our bags.
- ☐ 7 We arrived in Rome.
- ☐ We collected our tickets from the travel agent.
- ☐ 8 We went sightseeing.
- ☐ 9 We had a great time.

T 14.7 Listen and check.

5 Describe a journey in the past.

Where did you go?   How did you travel?   How long was the journey?

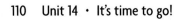

EVERYDAY ENGLISH
Going sightseeing

1 Write down the names of two cities and the dates when you were a tourist there.

London, July 1999.   Paris, April 2001.

Show a partner. Talk about the cities. What did you do there? What did you see? What did you buy?

- I went to ...
- I saw ...
- We visited ...
- I bought ...

2 **T 14.8**   Listen and complete the conversations in a tourist office.

1 **A** Hello. Can I _help you_?

   B Yes. _I would_ a map of the town, please.

   A _Here_ you are.

   B Thank you.

2 **C** We'd like _to go on_ a bus tour of _the city town_.

   A That's fine. The next _bus leaves_ at 10.00. It _takes_ an hour.

   C Where does the bus go from?

   A It _goes_ the _railway station_ in Princes Street.

3 **D** We'd like to visit the museum. _When is it_ open?

   A From ten o'clock to five o'clock _every day_.

   D _How much_ is it to get in?

   A It's free.

Practise the conversations.

What is there to do in your town? Where do visitors go?

> We have a beautiful church.

> There's a park.

> Visitors go to the market/ the old town ...

Work with a partner. One of you works in the Tourist Office in your town. The other is a tourist who wants some information.

A Hello. I'd like to go on a tour of the town/see the church ...

B That's fine ...

Tapescripts

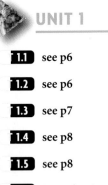

UNIT 1

1.1 see p6

1.2 see p6

1.3 see p7

1.4 see p8

1.5 see p8

1.6 Introductions

1 A Hello. My name's Anna. What's your name?
  B Ben.
2 C Hello. My name's Carla. What's your name?
  D My name's David.

1.7 Listen and check

1 B Hello, Anna. How are you?
  A Fine, thanks Ben. And you?
  B Very well, thanks.
2 D Hi, Carla. How are you?
  C Fine, thanks. And you?
  D OK, thanks.

1.8 Listen and number the lines

R Hello. My name's Rita. What's your name?
T I'm Tina, and this is Mary.
R Hello, Tina. Hello, Mary.
M Hello, Rita. How are you?
R I'm OK, thanks. And you?
M Fine, thanks.

1.9 see p10

T 1.10 see p10

1.11 see p11

T 1.12 Listen and check

ten sandwiches
two books
six bags
five computers
four houses
seven hamburgers
eight cameras
nine photographs
three cars
ten students

1.13 see p11

UNIT 2

T 2.1 see p12

T 2.2 see p12

T 2.3 see p12

T 2.4 Where are you from?

His name's Rick.
He's from the United States.
Her name's Sonia.
She's from Brazil.
His name's Jack.
He's from England.
His name's Sergio.
He's from Italy.
Her name's Marie.
She's from France.
Her name's Kim.
She's from Australia.

T 2.5 see p13

T 2.6 Cities and countries

Where's Tokyo?
It's in Japan.
Where's Paris?
It's in France.
Where's Barcelona?
It's in Spain.
Where's Milan?
It's in Italy.
Where's Oxford?
It's in England.
Where's Rio de Janeiro?
It's in Brazil.
Where's Boston?
It's in the United States.
Where's Sydney?
It's in Australia.

T 2.7 Questions and answers

S Hello, I'm Sandra. What's your name?
L My name's Luis.
S Hello, Luis. Where are you from?
L I'm from Spain. Where are *you* from?
S Oh, I'm from Spain, too. I'm from Madrid.

T 2.8 Listen and write

1 G Hello, I'm Gérard. I'm from France.
  A Hello, Gérard. I'm Akemi from Japan.
2 C Hello. My name's Charles. What's your name?
  B Hi, Charles. I'm Bud. I'm from the United States. Where are *you* from?
  C I'm from Oxford, in England.
  B Oh, yeah. I'm from Chicago.

3 L Hi, I'm Loretta. I'm from Sydney, Australia.
  J Hi, Loretta. I'm Jason. I'm from Australia, too.
  L Wow! Are you from Sydney?
  J No. I'm from Melbourne.

T 2.9 Listen and check

1 Where are you from?
  I'm from Brazil.
2 What's her name?
  Her name's Irena.
3 What's his name?
  His name's Luis.
4 Where's he from?
  He's from Madrid.
5 What's this in English?
  It's a computer.
6 How are you?
  Fine, thanks.
7 Where's Toronto?
  It's in Canada.

T 2.10 see p16

T 2.11 see p17

T 2.12 Listen and repeat

twenty-one
twenty-two
twenty-three
twenty-four
twenty-five
twenty-six
twenty-seven
twenty-eight
twenty-nine
thirty

T 2.13 Listen and tick

1 twelve
2 sixteen
3 twenty-one
4 seventeen
5 thirty

UNIT 3

T 3.1 Jobs

1 a teacher
2 a taxi driver
3 a police officer
4 a businessman
5 a doctor
6 a shop assistant
7 a nurse
8 a student

T 3.2 see p18

T 3.3 see p18

T 3.4 Listen and check

1 What's her name? Amy Roberts.
2 Where's she from? England.
3 What's her address?
  18, Market Street, Manchester.
4 What's her phone number?
  0161 929 5837.
5 How old is she? She's twenty.
6 What's her job? She's a student.
7 Is she married? No, she isn't.

T 3.5 see p19

T 3.6 Negatives and short answers

A Is your name Jeff?
J Yes, it is.
A Are you from England, Jeff?
J No, I'm not from England. I'm from Houston, Texas.
A Are you a police officer?
J Yes, I am.
A Are you 23?
J No, I'm not. I'm 25.
A Are you married?
J Yes, I am.

T 3.7 Giovanni Tomba and Diana Black

1 I Good morning.
  G Hello.
  I What's your name, please?
  G My name's Giovanni Tomba.
  I Thank you. And where are you from, Giovanni?
  G I'm from Rome, in Italy.
  I Thank you. And your telephone number, please?
  G 06 944 8139.
  I How old are you, Giovanni?
  G I'm twenty-three.
  I And … what's your job?
  G I'm a taxi driver.
  I And … are you married?
  G No, I'm not.
  I Thank you very much.

2 I Hello.
  D Hello.
  I What's your name, please?
  D Diana Black.
  I And where are you from?
  D From New York.
  I Ah! So you're from the United States.
  D Yes, I am.
  I What's your phone number?
  D 212 463 9145.
  I Thank you. How old are you?
  D I'm twenty-nine.
  I What's your job, Miss Black?
  D I'm a shop assistant.
  I And are you married?
  D Yes, I am.
  I That's fine. Thank you very much.

T 3.8 A pop group

I = Interviewer   C = Cath   G = George
M = Melanie   Y = Yves
I Hi!
All Hi!
I Now you're Melanie, yes?
M That's right.
I And you're from Australia.
M Uh huh.
I How old are you, Melanie?
M I'm 22.
I And Cath and George. You're from the United States, yeah?
G No, no. We aren't from the United States. We're from England.
I England. Sorry. How old are you both?
C I'm 21 and George is 20.
Y And I'm 19.
I Thanks. Now, who's married in *4x4*?
Y Well, I'm not married.
C and G We aren't married!
I Melanie, are you married?
M Yes, I am!
I Well, thank you, *4x4*. Welcome to New York!
All It's great here. Thanks!

T 3.9 Listen and check

1 A Good morning.
  B Good morning, Mr Brown.

2 A Good afternoon. The Grand Hotel.
  B Good afternoon.

3 A Good evening, madam.
  B Good evening.

4 A Good night.
  B Good night, Peter. Sleep well.

5 A Goodbye.
  B Goodbye. Have a good journey!

T 3.10 Listen and complete

1 A What's this in English?
  B I don't know.
  A It's a dictionary.

2 C *Hogy hívnak?*
  M I don't understand. Sorry.
  C What's your name?
  M My name's Manuel. I'm from Spain.

3 A The homework is on page … of the Workbook.
  B Pardon?
  A The homework is on page *thirty* of the Workbook.
  B Thank you.

UNIT 4

T 4.1 Listen and check

I, my
you, your
he, his
she, her
we, our
they, their

T 4.2 see p24

T 4.3 Listen and check

1 Is Sally married?
  Yes, she is.
2 Where's their house?
  It's in London.
3 What is Sally's job?
  She's a teacher.
4 Where's her school?
  It's in the centre of town.
5 What is Tom's job?
  He's a bank manager.
6 Where is his bank?
  It's in the centre of town.
7 Are their children doctors?
  No, they aren't. They're students.

T 4.4 Listen and repeat

mother
daughter
sister
wife

father
son
brother
husband

parents
children

T 4.5 Listen and complete

1 Sally is Tom's wife.
2 Tom is Sally's husband.
3 Kirsty is Sally and Tom's daughter.
4 Nick is their son.
5 Sally is Nick's mother.
6 Tom is Kirsty's father.
7 Kirsty is Nick's sister.
8 Nick is Kirsty's brother.
9 Sally and Tom are Kirsty and Nick's parents.
10 Kirsty and Nick are Tom and Sally's children.

T 4.6 The family

Hello! My name's Rachel, and I'm from the United States. This is a photo of my family. Our house is in San Diego. This is my brother. His name is Steve, and he's 15. He's a student. This is my mother. Her name's Grace. She's forty-two, and she's a doctor. And this man is my father, Bob. He's forty-four, and he's a businessman.

T 4.7 see p27

T 4.8 **Listen and write**

1 I have a small farm in Wales.
2 My wife has a job in town.
3 We have one son.
4 We have two dogs.
5 My sister and her husband have a house in London.
6 He has a very good job.
7 They have a son and a daughter.

T 4.9 **Listen and check**

1 How is your mother?
   She's very well, thank you.
2 What's your sister's job?
   She's a nurse.
3 How old are your brothers?
   They're ten and thirteen.
4 Who is Sally?
   She's David's sister.
5 Where is your office?
   It's in the centre of town.
6 Are you and your husband from Italy?
   Yes, we are.

T 4.10 see p30

T 4.11 **Write the names**

1 What's your name?
   Sally Milton.
   How do you spell your first name?
   S-A-L-L-Y.
   How do you spell your surname?
   M-I-L-T-O-N.
2 What's your name?
   Javier Ruiz.
   How do you spell your first name?
   J-A-V-I-E-R.
   How do you spell your surname?
   R-U-I-Z.
3 What's your name?
   Quentin Wexham.
   How do you spell your first name?
   Q-U-E-N-T-I-N.
   How do you spell your surname?
   W-E-X-H-A-M.
4 What's your name?
   Sumiko Matsuda.
   How do you spell your first name?
   S-U-M-I-K-O.
   How do you spell your surname?
   M-A-T-S-U-D-A.
5 What's your name?
   Fabien Leclerc.
   How do you spell your first name?
   F-A-B-I-E-N.
   How do you spell your surname?
   L-E-C-L-E-R-C.

T 4.12 see p31

 UNIT 5

T 5.1 see p32

T 5.2 see p33

T 5.3 **Bill**

Well, I like swimming and football – American football. I don't like tennis. Mmm yeah, hamburgers and pizza, I like hamburgers and pizza and Italian food, I like Italian food a lot, but not Chinese food – I don't like Chinese food and I don't like tea, but I like coffee and beer.

T 5.4 see p33

T 5.5 see p34

T 5.6 see p34

T 5.7 **Listen and complete**

W= a woman   G= Gordon

1 W Do you come from Scotland?
   G Yes, I do.
2 W Do you live in Aberdeen?
   G No, I don't. I live in London.
3 W Do you live in a flat?
   G Yes, I do. I live in a flat near the centre.
4 W Do you work in a Chinese restaurant?
   G No, I don't. I work in an Italian restaurant.
5 W Do you like Italian food?
   G Yes, I do. I like it a lot.
6 W Do you like your job?
   G No, I don't. I want to be an actor.
7 W Do you drink beer?
   G No, I don't. I don't like it.
8 W Do you speak French and Spanish?
   G I speak French but I don't speak Spanish.

T 5.8 see p35

T 5.9 **Languages and nationalities**

England	English
Germany	German
Italy	Italian
Mexico	Mexican
Brazil	Brazilian
Japan	Japanese
Portugal	Portuguese
China	Chinese
France	French
The United States	American
Spain	Spanish

T 5.10 **Listen and check**

1 In Brazil they speak Portuguese.
2 In Canada they speak English and French.
3 In France they speak French.
4 In Germany they speak German.
5 In Italy they speak Italian.
6 In Japan they speak Japanese.
7 In Mexico they speak Spanish.
8 In Portugal they speak Portuguese.
9 In Spain they speak Spanish.

10 In Switzerland they speak French, German, and Italian.
11 In the United States they speak English.

T 5.11 **Listen and check**

1 an American car
2 German beer
3 Spanish oranges
4 a Japanese camera
5 Mexican food
6 an English dictionary
7 an Italian bag
8 Brazilian coffee
9 French wine

T 5.12 **At a party**

A = Alessandra   W= Woody

A Hello. I'm Alessandra.
W Hi, Alessandra. I'm Woody. Woody Bates.
A Do you live here in London, Woody?
W No, I don't. I work in London but I live in Brighton.
A What's your job?
W I'm an actor. What's your job?
A I work in a hotel.
W You aren't English, but you speak English very well. Where do you come from?
A I'm Italian. I come from Verona.
W Oh, I love Italy.
A Really?
W Oh, yes. I like the food and the wine very much.

T 5.13 see p39

T 5.14 see p39

T 5.15 see p39

T 5.16 **Listen and tick**

1 The cheese sandwich is 90p.
2 The football is £14.
3 The camera is £90.99.
4 The beer is £1.60.
5 The chocolate is 60p.
6 The mobile phone is £24.74.
7 The dictionary is £10.75.
8 The bag is £30.99.

 UNIT 6

T 6.1 **Listen and repeat**

1 It's nine o'clock.
2 It's nine thirty.
3 It's nine forty-five.
4 It's ten o'clock.
5 It's ten fifteen.
6 It's two o'clock.
7 It's two thirty.
8 It's two forty-five.
9 It's three o'clock.
10 It's three fifteen.

T 6.2 see p40

6.3 Lena's schooldays

Well, on schooldays I get up at seven forty-five. I have breakfast at eight and I go to school at eight thirty. I have lunch in school with my friends, that's at twelve fifteen – it's early in our school. I leave school at three thirty in the afternoon and I walk home with my friends. I get home at four thirty. I go to bed at eleven o'clock on schooldays, but not at the weekend.

6.4 see p41

6.5 Listen and repeat

1 gets up
  has a shower
2 has breakfast
3 leaves home
  goes to work
4 has lunch
5 works late
  leaves work
6 buys
  eats
  gets home
7 goes out
  works
8 goes to bed

6.6 Listen and repeat

He usually works late.
He sometimes buys a pizza.
He never goes out in the evening.

6.7 Questions and negatives

1 What time does he get up?
  He gets up at six o'clock.
2 When does he go to bed?
  He goes to bed at eleven forty-five.
3 Does he go to work by taxi?
  Yes, he does.
4 Does he have lunch in a restaurant?
  No, he doesn't.
5 Does he go out in the evening?
  No, he doesn't.

6.8 Listen and check

1 What time does he have breakfast?
  He has breakfast at six forty-five.
2 When does he leave home?
  He leaves home at seven fifteen.
3 Does he go to work by bus?
  No, he doesn't. He goes to work by taxi.
4 Where does he have lunch?
  He has lunch in his office.
5 Does he usually work late?
  Yes, he does.
6 Does he eat in a restaurant?
  No, he doesn't. He sometimes buys a pizza and eats it at home.
7 What does he do in the evening?
  He works at his computer.

6.9 Katya's day

Katya is twenty-five. She's an artist. She lives in a small house in the country. She usually gets up at ten o'clock in the morning. She never gets up early. She has coffee and toast for breakfast and then she goes for a walk with her dog. She gets home at eleven o'clock and she paints in her studio until seven o'clock in the evening. Then she cooks dinner and drinks a glass of wine. After dinner, she sometimes listens to music and she sometimes plays the piano. She usually goes to bed very late, at one or two o'clock in the morning.

6.10 Negatives and pronunciation

1 She doesn't live in the town. She lives in the country.
2 He doesn't get up at ten o'clock. He gets up at six o'clock.
3 She doesn't have a big breakfast. She has coffee and toast.
4 He doesn't have a dog. She has a dog.
5 She doesn't work in an office. She works at home.
6 He doesn't cook dinner in the evening. He buys a pizza.
7 She doesn't go to bed early. She goes to bed late.
8 They don't go out in the evening. They stay at home.

6.11 Words that go together

get up early
go to bed late
listen to music
watch TV
cook dinner
work in an office

go shopping
have a shower
eat in restaurants
drink beer
play the piano
stay at home

6.12 see p46

6.13 Days of the week

Monday, Tuesday, Wednesday, Thursday, Friday, Saturday, Sunday

6.14 Listen and check

on Sunday
on Monday
on Tuesday
on Saturday evening
on Thursday morning
on Friday afternoon

at nine o'clock
at ten thirty
at twelve fifteen
at the weekend

in the morning
in the afternoon
in the evening

T 7.1 Match the questions and answers

1 What is the capital of Australia?
  Canberra.
2 How old are the Pyramids?
  4,500 years old.
3 What time do Spanish people have dinner?
  Late. At 10.00 in the evening.
4 Where does the American President live?
  In the White House.
5 How many floors does the Empire State Building have?
  86.
6 How much is a hamburger in the US?
  $3.50.
7 Who lives in Buckingham Palace?
  The Queen of England.

T 7.2 I love it here!

C = Céline   G = Guy
G This is a very beautiful house.
C Thank you. I like it very much, too.
G Céline, you're American. Why do you live here in London?
C Because I just love it here! The people are fantastic! I love them! And of course, my husband, Charles, is English, and I love him, too!
G That's a very nice photo. Who are they?
C My sons. That's Matt, and that's Jack. They go to school here. My daughter's at school in the US. Her name's Lisa-Marie.
G Why does Lisa-Marie go to school in the US?
C Because she lives with her father. My first husband, you know, the actor Dan Brat. I hate him and all his movies. I never watch them.
G I see. And does Lisa-Marie visit you?
C Oh, yes. She visits me every vacation. She's here with me now.
G And is this a photo of you and Charles?
C Oh yes. It's us in Hawaii. It's our wedding. We're so happy together!

T 7.3 I like them!

1 Do you like ice-cream?
  Yes, I love it.
2 Do you like dogs?
  No, I hate them.
3 Do you like me?
  Of course I like you!
4 Does your teacher teach you French?
  No, she teaches us English.
5 Do you like your teacher?
  We like her very much.

T 7.4 Questions and answers

1 Why does Céline drink champagne?
  Because she likes it.
2 Why do you eat oranges?
  Because I like them.
3 Why does Annie want to marry Peter?
  Because she loves him.
4 Why do you eat Chinese food?
  Because I like it.

5 Why don't you like your maths teacher?
  Because he gives us a lot of homework.
6 Why does Miguel buy presents for Maria?
  Because he loves her.

T 7.5 Listen and check
1 How do you come to school?
  By bus.
2 What do you have for breakfast?
  Toast and coffee.
3 Who is your favourite pop group?
  I don't have a favourite. I like a lot.
4 Where does your father work?
  In an office in the centre of town.
5 Why do you want to learn English?
  Because it's an international language.
6 How much money do you have in your bag?
  Not a lot. About two pounds.
7 When do lessons start at your school?
  They start at nine o'clock.
8 How many languages does your teacher speak?
  Three.

T 7.6 Adjectives
1 It's lovely.
2 It's horrible.
3 They're old.
4 They're new.
5 It's big.
6 It's small.
7 He's hot.
8 She's cold.
9 They're expensive.
10 They're cheap.

T 7.7 see p53

T 7.8 Keiko in town
1 A Yes, please!
  K Can I have a ham sandwich, please?
  A OK.
  K How much is that?
  A Two pounds ninety, please.
  K There you are.
  A Thanks a lot.
2 K Hello. Can I try on this jumper, please?
  B Of course. The changing rooms are
    just here.
3 K Can I send an email, please?
  C OK. PC number two.
  K How much is it?
  C 1p a minute. Pay at the end, please.
4 D Good morning. Can I help you?
  K Yes, please. Can I change this traveller's
    cheque?
  D How much is it?
  K Fifty dollars.
  D OK.
5 K Can I buy a return ticket to Oxford, please?
  E Sure.
  K How much is that?
  E Twenty-two pounds fifty, please.
  K Thank you.
  E Twenty-five pounds. Here's your ticket,
    and £2.50 change.

 UNIT 8

T 8.1 Listen and repeat
living room
dining room
kitchen
bedroom
bathroom
toilet

T 8.2 see p56

T 8.3 Nicole's living room
My living room isn't very big, but I love it.
There's a sofa, and there are two armchairs.
There's a small table with a TV on it, and there
are a lot of books. There's a CD player, and
there are some CDs. There are pictures on the
wall, and there are two lamps. It's a very
comfortable room.

T 8.4 see p57

T 8.5 Prepositions
1 Nicole's mobile phone is on the bed.
2 The magazine is next to the phone.
3 Her CD player is on the floor next to the
  bed.
4 Her car keys are in the drawer.
5 Her bag is on the floor under the chair.
6 The books are under her bed.

T 8.6 Listen and check
1 Do you live in a house or a flat?
2 How many bedrooms are there?
3 Is there a telephone in the kitchen?
4 Is there a television in the living room?
5 Is there a video recorder under the television?
6 Are there a lot of books in your bedroom?
7 Are there any pictures on the wall?

T 8.7
There's a cat on the sofa and there's a
telephone on a small table next to the sofa.
There's a CD player with some CDs under it.
Not a lot of CDs. There isn't a television and
there aren't any pictures or photographs on
the walls. There's one lamp, it's next to the
table with the telephone. There are two tables
and two armchairs. There are some books
under one of the tables.

T 8.8 Sydney
How to have a good time in … Sydney
Sydney has everything you want in a city. It's
beautiful, it has old and new buildings, there
are fantastic beaches, and the food is delicious.
When to go
The best times to visit are spring and autumn.
In summer it is very hot.
Where to stay
There are cheap hotels in King's Cross. A room is
about $50 a night. There are international hotels
in the centre. Here a room is about $150 a night.
What to do
Sydney has theatres and cinemas, and of course,
the Opera House. The best shops are in Pitt Street.

Go to the harbour. There are beaches, walks,
parks, and cafés and, of course, the wonderful
bridge.
Sydney has the famous Bondi Beach. People go
swimming, surfing, windsurfing, and sailing.
For night-life, there are clubs and bars in
Oxford Street.
What to eat
There are restaurants from every country –
Italian, Turkish, Lebanese, Japanese, Thai,
Chinese, and Vietnamese. Australians eat a lot
of seafood – it's very fresh!
How to travel
There are fast trains and slow buses. The best
way to see Sydney is by ferry.

T 8.9 My home town
G'day! My name is Darren, and I live in a house
with my brother and a friend. We live in Bondi
and we all love surfing. We often go surfing in
the morning before work.
I'm an engineer. I work in the centre of Sydney
for a big international company. I go to work
by train. My office is in Macarthur Street, very
near the Harbour. On Monday, Wednesday, and
Friday I go running at lunchtime. It's very hot in
summer, but it's beautiful. I sometimes go with
friends from work. We run near the Opera House.
My girlfriend likes to go shopping on Saturday.
There is a great market in Paddington, and there
are some great clothes shops in Oxford Street.
On Saturday night, we often go to Chinatown.
The food is fantastic, and really cheap. Or we
stay in Bondi because there are a lot of really
good little Thai and Italian restaurants here.
I usually relax on Sunday. When the weather is
good, we go to the beach, Manly Beach.
We go by ferry. When it's wet, we go to the pub.

T 8.10 Directions
1 Go down King's Road. Turn right at the
  Grand Hotel into Charles Street. It's next to
  the cinema.
2 Go straight on, past Charles Street and past
  Park Lane. It's on the left, next to the
  supermarket.
3 Go down King's Road. Turn right at the
  church. Go down Station Road. It's a big
  building on the right.
4 Go down King's Road. Turn left at the bank
  into Charles Street. It's on the right, next to
  the theatre.
5 Go straight on. It's on King's Road, on the
  left, next to the post office.

 UNIT 9

T 9.1 Listen and underline
1 fourteen twenty-six
2 seventeen ninety-nine
3 eighteen eighty
4 nineteen thirty-nine
5 nineteen sixty-one
6 two thousand and seven

9.2 see p64

 9.3 When were they born?

Leonardo da Vinci was a painter and scientist.
He was born in 1452 in Tuscany, Italy.
Marie Curie was a scientist. She was born in
1867 in Warsaw, Poland.

9.4 see p65

9.5 see p65

9.6 Calico Jones

My name's Calico. I know, it's a funny name! I
was born in 1987. My two brothers are Henry
and William, they were born… er … Henry in
1992 and William just one year later in 1993.
Ugh – they're horrible! My little sister is Cleo,
she's OK. She was born in 1999. Mum and dad
are Linda and Alan. My mum was born in
1961 and my dad … er … I think he was born
in 1961, too. And my grandmother … er, she
was born in 1930 something … yes, 1932. Her
name's Violet. I think it's a beautiful name.

9.7 Listen and write

1 Shakespeare was born in England in 1564.
2 Van Gogh was born in Holland in 1853.
3 Beethoven was born in Germany in 1770.
4 Marilyn Monroe was born in the US in 1926.
5 Elvis Presley was born in the US in 1935.
6 Diana Spencer was born in England in 1961.
7 Ayrton Senna was born in Brazil in 1960.
8 Indira Gandhi was born in India in 1917.

9.8 see p66

9.9 see p67

T 9.10 Listen, check, and repeat

1 Ayrton Senna was an actor.
  No, he wasn't. He was a racing driver.
2 Marie Curie was a princess.
  No, she wasn't. She was a scientist.
3 Marilyn Monroe and Elvis Presley were
  Italian.
  No, they weren't. They were American.
4 Beethoven was a scientist.
  No, he wasn't. He was a musician.
5 Leonardo da Vinci and Van Gogh were
  musicians.
  No, they weren't. They were painters.
6 Indira Gandhi was a singer.
  No, she wasn't. She was a politician.

T 9.11 Past Simple – irregular verbs

are	were
is	was
buy	bought
go	went
say	said
see	saw
take	took

T 9.12 We're millionaires!

In August 1999 three friends, Jacques Proust, Guy
Fadat, and François Leclerc, were on holiday in
the town of Laraque in France. On Sunday they
went shopping in the market and they saw a
dirty, old painting of the Virgin Mary. They
bought it for 1,400 francs and they took it to
Paris. In Paris, an expert said that the painting
was by Leonardo da Vinci and it was worth
500,000,000 francs. The man in Laraque market
said: 'I was happy to sell the painting but now
I'm very upset. I don't want to think about it!'

T 9.13 Months of the year

January, February, March, April, May, June,
July, August, September, October, November,
December

T 9.14 see p70

T 9.15 see p71

T 9.16 Listen and write

the first of January
the third of March
the seventh of April
the twentieth of May
the second of June
the twelfth of August
the fifteenth of November
the thirty-first of December

UNIT 10

T 10.1 Listen, check, and repeat

1 We're at school now.
2 You were at home yesterday.
3 I went to Australia in 1997.
4 She lives in London now.
5 They bought their house in 1997.
6 It was cold and wet yesterday.

T 10.2 Betsy

Yesterday was Sunday, so I got up late, eleven
thirty. I had a big breakfast, orange juice, toast,
eggs, and coffee. Then I went shopping, to the
supermarket, and I bought some chocolate and
a Sunday newspaper, the *Sunday Times*. In the
afternoon I listened to music for a bit and then
I watched a film on TV. In the evening I cooked
a meal just for me, not a big meal, just soup
and a salad. I went to bed early. It was a lovely,
lazy day.

T 10.3 Listen and repeat

work	worked
watch	watched
cook	cooked
play	played
stay	stayed
listen	listened

T 10.4

visit	visited
want	wanted
hate	hated

T 10.5 Betsy and Dan

B = Betsy   D = Dan

B Hi, Dan. Did you have a good weekend?
D Yes, I did, thanks.
B What did you do yesterday?
D Well, yesterday morning I got up early and
  I played tennis with some friends.
B You got up early on Sunday!
D I know, I know. I don't usually get up early
  on Sunday.
B Did you go out yesterday afternoon?
D No, I didn't. I just stayed at home. I watched
  the football on TV.
B Ugh, football! What did you do yesterday
  evening?
D Oh, I didn't do much. I worked a bit at my
  computer. I didn't go to bed late. About
  11.00.

T 10.6 Listen and check

1 B Did you have a good weekend?
  D Yes, I did.
2 B What did you do yesterday?
  D I played tennis.
3 B Did you go out yesterday afternoon?
  D No, I didn't.
4 B What did you do yesterday evening?
  D I didn't do much. I didn't go to bed late.

T 10.7 Listen and repeat

A Did you get up early?
B Yes, I did.
A Did she get up early?
B No, she didn't.
We didn't go to work.
They didn't go to work.

T 10.8 Did you have a good weekend?

1 A I went to the cinema.
  B What did you see?
2 A I went shopping.
  B What did you buy?
3 A I had a meal in a restaurant.
  B What did you have?
4 A I saw my friends.
  B Who did you see?
5 A I played football.
  B Where did you play?
6 A I went to a party.
  B What time did you leave?
7 A I did my homework.
  B How much homework did you do?
8 A I did the housework.
  B How much housework did you do?

T 10.9 see p75

T 10.10 Listen and check

1 Do you work in New York?
  No, I don't.
2 Did she like the film?
  Yes, she did.
3 Does he watch TV every evening?
  Yes, he does.
4 Did you go out yesterday evening?
  No, we didn't.

5 Did he go to the party?
  Yes, he did.

6 Do you buy a newspaper every morning?
  Yes, I do.

7 Does she usually go to bed late?
  No, she doesn't.

8 Did they have a good time?
  No, they didn't.

T 10.11 Holidays

C = Colin   F = Fran

C Well, usually we go on holiday in summer.
F Yes, and usually we go to Spain … but last year we …
C … last year we went to Switzerland, and we went in winter.
F We stayed in a chalet and we cooked all our own meals there. It was lovely.
C Yes, in Spain we usually stay in a hotel and eat in restaurants.
F It was good to do different things too. Usually we just go swimming and sit in the sun …
C And I sometimes play golf. I love that!
F Ah yes, you do. But of course in Switzerland we went skiing every day, and sometimes we went ice-skating in the afternoons – it was great fun.
C And in the evenings we cooked a meal and then played cards. We had a very good time.
F We love holidays – we always have a good time in Spain too.

T 10.12 Listen and check

1 Last year Colin and Fran didn't go on holiday in summer. They went in winter.
2 They didn't go to Spain. They went to Switzerland.
3 They didn't stay in a hotel. They stayed in a chalet.
4 They didn't eat in restaurants. They cooked their own meals.
5 They didn't go swimming. They went skiing.

UNIT 11

T 11.1 What can they do?

1 Josh is a schoolboy. He can use a computer.
2 Sharon is an athlete. She can run fast.
3 Lucy is an architect. She can draw well.
4 Ted is an interpreter. He can speak French and German.
5 Archie is a farmer. He can drive a tractor.
6 Mabel is a grandmother. She can make cakes.

T 11.2 see p81

T 11.3 see p81

T 11.4 Josh

T = Tessa   J = Josh

T Can you use a computer, Josh?
J Yes, of course I can. All my friends can. I use a computer at school and at home.
T That's very good. What other things can you do?
J Well, I can run fast, very fast, and I can draw a bit. I can draw planes and cars very well but I can't drive a car of course. When I'm big I want to be a farmer and drive a tractor.
T And I know you can speak French.
J Yes, I can. I can speak French very well because my dad's French. We sometimes speak French at home.
T Can you speak any other languages?
J No, I can't. I can't speak German or Spanish, just French – and English of course! And I can cook! I can make cakes. My grandma makes lovely cakes and I sometimes help her. Yesterday we made a big chocolate cake.

T 11.5 Pronunciation

1 I can use a computer.
2 She can't speak German.
3 He can speak English very well.
4 Why can't you come to my party?
5 We can't understand our teacher.
6 They can read music.
7 Can we have an ice-cream?
8 Can't cats swim?

T 11.6 Tito

I come from South America, from Argentina, but now I live and work in England, in London. I can speak four languages – Spanish, of course, French, German, and English. I can speak English very well now but in the beginning it was very difficult for me. I can drive a car and I can ride a horse – I don't ride in London but when I'm back home in Argentina I ride. I can't ski and I can't cook very well and I can't play the piano – but I can play the guitar.

T 11.7 Requests and offers

1 Can you tell me the time, please?
  It's about three thirty.

2 Can you speak more slowly, please?
  I'm sorry. Can you understand now?

3 Can you come to my party?
  I'm sorry. I can't. It's my grandma's birthday.

4 Can I help you?
  Yes, please. I want to buy this postcard.

5 Can I have a cold drink, please?
  Yes, of course. Do you want Coca-Cola or orange juice?

T 11.8 see p85

T 11.9 Listen to the people

1 Fleur
I use the Internet a lot. Every day, I think. It helps me with my homework. It helps me with everything. Yesterday I did an English test. It was quite difficult.

2 Anya
My brother's in Japan. I can't phone Japan, it's very expensive – so Paul (that's my brother) and me – we 'talk' in chat rooms on the Internet. We talk late, at about 11 o'clock in the evening – well, it's evening here, but it's eight o'clock in the morning in Japan.

3 Tito
I play the guitar and I can find lots of songs on the Internet. Yesterday I got the words and music for *Can't buy me love*, you know, by the Beatles. I can play it now. I use the Internet at weekends because it's cheap then.

4 Henry
Well, my family's name is Krum and I want to write about my family, so every day I chat to people from all over the world, Canada, Germany, Argentina – people who have the name Krum. They send me information about their families. It's really interesting.

5 Tommy
I play games. And I go to chat rooms. And I go on websites for my favourite pop groups and football players. I want to be on the web all the time, but my mum says I can't. She says I can only use it after school for an hour, and then I stop.

6 Iris
I go shopping on the Internet. Every Friday I go to my son's house and I use his computer. It's fantastic – the supermarket brings all my shopping to my home.

T 11.10 What's the problem?

1 A Come on! It's time to go to the airport.
  B But I can't find my passport.
  A You put it in your bag.
  B Did I? Oh, yes. Here it is! Phew!

2 A Excuse me!
  B Yes?
  A This ticket machine doesn't work. I put in two pounds, but I didn't get a ticket.
  B Did you push this button?
  A Oh! No, I didn't.
  B Ah, well. Here you are.
  A Thank you very much.

3 A Excuse me.
  B Yes?
  A Can you help me! I'm lost.
  B Where do you want to go?
  A To the railway station.
  B Go straight on. About two hundred metres. It's on your left.

4 A I don't understand this word.
  B Check it in your dictionary.
  A My dictionary's at home. Can I borrow yours?
  B OK. No problem. Here you are.

5 A Oh no!
  B What's the matter?
  A The TV's broken.
  B Good! Perhaps we can talk this evening.
  A But I want to watch a film.
  B Go to the cinema, then.

6 **A** I'm really sorry. I forgot your birthday.
   B It doesn't matter.
   A It was on the tenth, wasn't it?
   B Yes, it was.
   A Well, here are some flowers.
   B Oh, thank you very much. They're beautiful.

UNIT 12

T 12.1 Listen and check
You can buy stamps in a post office.
You can buy a dictionary in a book shop.
You can buy a computer magazine in a newsagent.
You can change money in a bank.
You can buy a CD in a music shop.
You can get a cup of coffee in a café.
You can send an email in an Internet café.

T 12.2 A trip into town
E = Enrique
1 **E** Good morning. I'd like a stamp for this letter to Venezuela, please.
   A That's 75p.
   E Thank you.
   A Here you are, and 25p change.
   E Thanks a lot. Bye.
2 **E** I'd like a cup of coffee, please.
   B Would you like black or white?
   E Black, please.
   B All right. Here you are. One pound twenty, please.
3 **E** Hello. I'd like to buy a Spanish/English dictionary.
   C OK. Would you like a big dictionary or a minidictionary?
   E Just a minidictionary, please.
   C This one is £4.99.
   E That's fine. Thank you very much.

T 12.3 see p89

T 12.4 Where is Enrique?
E = Enrique
1 **A** Can I help you?
   E Yes. I'd like the new CD by Gary Alright, please.
   A There you are.
   E How much is that?
   A £11.99.
   E Thank you very much.
2 **E** I'd like to send an email, please.
   B Take PC number ten.
   E Thanks a lot.
3 **E** Hello. I'd like this month's PC Worldwide magazine, please.
   C Here you are. That's £2.20, please.
   E Thank you very much. Bye.
4 **E** Two tickets for James Bond, please.
   D Eight pounds forty, please.
   E Thanks. What time does the film start?
   D Seven thirty.
   E Thanks very much.

5 **F** Good afternoon. Can I help you?
   E Yes, please. I'd like to change some traveller's cheques, please.
   F Certainly. Are they in American dollars?
   E Yes, they are.
   F Fine. That's £115 and 25p.
   E Thank you very much.

T 12.5 It's my birthday!
Suzanne
What would I like for my birthday? That's easy. I'd like to have breakfast in bed. With the newspapers. And in the evening I'd like to go to the theatre.

Tom
Well, I'd like a new computer, because my computer is so old that the new programs don't work on it. And then in the evening, I'd like to go to a good restaurant. I don't mind if it's Italian, French, Chinese, or Indian. Just good food.

Alice
I don't have a mobile phone, and all my friends have one, so what I'd really like is my own mobile. They aren't expensive these days. And in the evening, I'd like to go out with all my friends and have a great time!

T 12.6 Listening and pronunciation
1 Would you like a Coke?
2 I like orange juice.
3 We'd like to go for a walk.
4 What do you like doing at the weekend?
5 We like our new car.

T 12.7 see p92

T 12.8 Joe's Diner
W = Waiter   P = Paul   R = Renate
W Are you ready to order?
P Yes, we are. Renate, what would you like to start?
R Can I have the tomato soup, please?
P And I'd like the seafood cocktail.
W And for your main course?
R I would like the er … roast chicken, please.
W Certainly. And for you?
P Can I have the steak, please?
W How would you like it cooked?
P Medium.
W What would you like to drink?
P Can we have a bottle of red wine, please?
W Very good.
R And we'd like a bottle of mineral water, too.
W Thank you very much.
(Pause)
W Is everything all right?
R Delicious, thank you.

T 12.9 She only eats junk food
1 When was Mary Alston's birthday?
   It was yesterday.
2 Did she have a party?
   Yes, she did.
3 Does she eat fresh food?
   No, she doesn't.
4 What does she eat?
   Popcorn, pizza, and burgers.

5 What was her job?
   She was a teacher.
6 Where was she born?
   On a farm in Pennsylvania.
7 When did she marry?
   She married in 1915.
8 What time does she get up?
   She gets up at six o'clock.
9 Where does she go every Friday?
   She goes to the hairdresser.
10 What did she say to her granddaughter?
   'I'd like a cheeseburger and fries!'

T 12.10 Going shopping
1 **A** Excuse me! Where can I buy a film for my camera?
   B In a chemist.
   A Is there a chemist near here?
   B Yes, two hundred metres from here, next to the bank.
2 **C** Can I help you?
   A No, thanks. I'm just looking.
3 **A** Excuse me! Do you have this shirt in a medium?
   C No, I'm sorry. That's all we have.
4 **A** I'd like to try on a pair of jeans, please.
   C Sure. What size are you?
   A I think I'm a forty.
   C Fine. The changing rooms are over there.
5 **D** Yes, madam. What would you like?
   A I'd like a kilo of potatoes, please.
   D Anything else?
   A No, that's all, thanks. How much is that?
6 **A** Excuse me! Do you sell Spanish newspapers?
   E No, I'm sorry, we don't.
   A Where can I buy them?
   E Try the railway station.

UNIT 13

T 13.1 Listen and check
1 George's jacket is black. Sadie's jacket is red.
2 His trousers are grey. Her trousers are green.
3 Her shirt is yellow. His shirt is white.
4 Her shoes are blue. His shoes are brown.

T 13.2 see p97

T 13.3 see p97

T 13.4 Listen and check
1 He's cooking.
2 He's driving.
3 He's having a shower.
4 She's writing.
5 She's skiing.
6 She's eating an ice-cream.
7 They're running.
8 They're dancing.
9 They're playing football.

T 13.5 see p98

T 13.6 Asking questions

1 A What are you reading?
   B A love story.

2 A What are you watching?
   B The news.

3 A Where are you going?
   B To my bedroom.

4 A Why are you wearing three jumpers?
   B Because I'm cold.

5 A What are you eating?
   B Chocolate.

6 A How many cakes are you making?
   B Five.

7 A Who are you talking to?
   B My girlfriend.

T 13.7 see p102

T 13.8 Listen and complete

1 She has long, fair hair.
2 He has short, black hair.
3 She has blue eyes.
4 He has brown eyes.

T 13.9 What's the matter?

1 She's cold.
2 He's hungry.
3 They're tired.
4 He's thirsty.
5 They're hot.
6 She's bored.

T 13.10 see p103

UNIT 14

T 14.1 Ellie's holiday plans

I'm going on holiday to Mexico next Friday, so next week's very busy. On Monday I'm collecting my tickets from the travel agent. I'm going on holiday with my friends Ed and Lucy, so on Tuesday I'm meeting them after work and we're going shopping. On Wednesday I'm seeing the doctor at eleven o'clock, then I'm having lunch with mum. On Thursday I'm leaving work early and I'm packing. I'm taking just a bag and a rucksack. Then it's Friday. Friday's the big day! At six thirty in the morning I'm going by taxi to the airport. I'm meeting Ed and Lucy there and at nine thirty we're flying to Mexico City. I'm very excited!

T 14.2 see p105

T 14.3 Listen and check

A What are you doing?
E I'm reading about Mexico.
A Why?
E Because I'm going there on holiday soon.
A Oh lovely! When are you leaving?
E We're leaving next Friday.
A Who are you going with?

E My friends Ed and Lucy.
A How are you travelling?
E We're travelling by plane to Mexico City, then by bus and train around the country.
A Where are you staying?
E We're staying in small hotels and hostels.
A You're so lucky! Have a good time!
E Thanks very much.

T 14.4 Marco's holiday plans

A Marco's going on holiday.
B Oh, where's he going?
A To Banff, in Canada.
B Why is he going there?
A Because it's good for skiing and he wants to go skiing.
B When is he leaving?
A Next week on the third of March.
B How is he travelling?
A By plane to Vancouver and then by train to Banff.
B Where is he staying?
A In the Banff Springs Hotel.
B And how long is he staying?
A Just ten days.

T 14.5 Listen, check, and repeat

1 I got up early.
  Are you getting up early tomorrow?

2 I went swimming.
  Are you going swimming tomorrow?

3 I walked to work.
  Are you walking to work tomorrow?

4 I had lunch in my office.
  Are you having lunch in your office tomorrow?

5 I left work late.
  Are you leaving work late tomorrow?

6 I met a friend.
  Are you meeting a friend tomorrow?

7 We had dinner in a restaurant.
  Are you having dinner in a restaurant tomorrow?

T 14.6 An amazing journey

JP = John Pollard   I = Interviewer
I This is an amazing car, John. When did you buy it?
JP In 1964, when I was a student.
I And how much did it cost?
JP £505.
I Why did you buy it?
JP Because I wanted to travel. In 1966 I drove to Moscow, Finland, and the Arctic Circle.
I Does your wife like the Mini?
JP Oh, yes. She loves it. We married in 1967 and we drove to Australia via India. We stayed in Australia for over thirty years.
I When did you come back to England?
JP Last month.
I Are you going back to Australia?
JP Yes, we are. We're flying back next month.
I Are you leaving the Mini in England?
JP No, we aren't. The Mini is travelling by ship.

T 14.7 Transport and travel

1 We wanted to have a holiday in Rome.
2 We booked the hotel and the flight.
3 We collected our tickets from the travel agent.
4 We packed our bags.
5 We went to the airport.
6 We caught the plane.
7 We arrived in Rome.
8 We went sightseeing.
9 We had a great time.

T 14.8 Going sightseeing

1 A Hello. Can I help you?
   B Yes. I'd like a map of the town, please.
   A Here you are.
   B Thank you.

2 C We'd like to go on a bus tour of the city.
   A That's fine. The next bus leaves at ten. It takes an hour.
   C Where does the bus go from?
   A It goes from the railway station in Princes Street.

3 D We'd like to visit the museum. When is it open?
   A From ten o'clock to five o'clock every day.
   D How much is it to get in?
   A It's free.

Grammar Reference

1.1 *am/are/is*

I	'm am	John Mason. fine.
You	're are	Hiro.
My name	's is	Sandra.
This	is	

1.2 Questions with question words

What's your name?   *what's = what is*
How are you?

1.3 Possessive adjectives

My name's John.
What's **your** name?

1.4 Plural nouns

1 Most nouns add *-s.*
    book   books
    computer   computer**s**
    camera   camera**s**

2 Some nouns add *-es.*
    sandwich   sandwich**es**

2.1 *am/are/is*

I	'm (am)	
You	're (are)	very well. a student. from Japan.
He She	's (is)	

2.2 Possessive adjectives

His name's Juan.
What's **her** name?

My name's Maria.
What's **your** name?

❶ *his* = possessive adjective
his name, his car, his camera

he's = he is
He's Bruno. He's from Italy. He's fine.

2.3 Questions with question words

Where	are you is she is he	from?
What	's your (is your) 's her (is her)	name?

2.4 *am/are/is*

I'm (am)	
You're (are)	from England. a student.
He's She's (is) It's	fine. in Paris. in New York.
They're (are)	married.

3.1 *am/are/is*

Negative

I	'm not (am not)	a teacher.
He She	isn't (is not)	from Spain. married. very well.

Yes/No **questions and short answers**

Are you married?	Yes, I am. No, I'm not.
Is she a teacher?	Yes, she is. No, she isn't.
Is he English?	Yes, he is. No, he isn't.
Is her name Alice?	Yes, it is. No, it isn't.

3.2 *am/are/is* (verb *to be*)

Positive

I	'm (am)	
He She It	's (is)	from the USA.
You We They	're (are)	

Negative

I	'm not	
He She It	isn't	English.
You We They	aren't	

Questions with question words

		Answers
What	is your name? is her address? is his phone number?	John Mason. 16, Albert Road, Bristol. 01693 456729.
Where	are you from? is he from? are they from?	From Spain.
How old	are you? are they?	I'm 16. They're 8 and 10.

Yes/No **questions**

			Short answers
Is	he she it	American?	Yes, he is. No, she isn't. Yes, it is.
Are	you we they	married?	Yes, I am. No, we aren't. No, they aren't.

UNIT 4

4.1 Possessive adjectives

	my your his	
This is	her our their	book.

4.2 Possessive 's

's shows possession.

my son	→	John's son
your job	→	Marie's job
his house	→	Tom's house
her name	→	your wife's name

❶ *'s* is also the short form of *is*.

he's	=	he is
she's	=	she is
it's	=	it is
Who's	=	Who is

4.3 Plural nouns

1 Most nouns add *-s* in the plural.

doctor	→	doctors
book	→	books
student	→	students

2 Nouns that end in *-s*, *-ss*, *-sh*, or *ch* add *-es*.

bus	→	buses
class	→	classes
sandwich	→	sandwiches

3 Some nouns that end in *-y* change to *-ies*.

city	→	cities
country	→	countries
dictionary	→	dictionaries

4 Some nouns are irregular.

man	→	men
woman	→	women
child	→	children

4.4 have/has

Have is an irregular verb.

I You We They	have	a good job. a computer.
He She It	has	

UNIT 5

5.1 Present Simple – *I / you / we / they*

Positive

I You We They	like coffee. play tennis. live in London. speak two languages. have a good job.

Negative

I You We They	don't	like tennis. speak French. work in a restaurant.

Questions with question words

Where		you live?
What sports	do	we like?
How many languages		they speak?

***Yes/No* questions and short answers**

Do you like football?	Yes, I do. No, I don't.
Do they speak English?	Yes, they do. No, they don't.

❶ Do you like tea?   Yes, I do.   NOT   ~~Yes, I like.~~

5.2 a/an

We use *an* before words that begin with *a*, *e*, *i*, *o*, and *u*.

an actor
an English dictionary
an ice-cream
an orange
an umbrella

but

a car
a hamburger
a television

5.3 adjective + noun   *PRIDAVNE MENO 1+NO*

Adjectives always come *before* the noun.

an **American** car		~~a car American~~
a **Japanese** camera	NOT	~~a camera Japanese~~
a **beautiful** girl		~~a girl beautiful~~

❶ Spanish oranges   NOT   ~~Spanishes oranges~~

6.1 Present Simple *he / she / it*   PRITOMNÝ ČAS

Positive

He She	gets up	at 8.00.
It	leaves	

6.2 Spelling – Present Simple *he / she / it*

1 Most verbs add -*s*.
   he   listen**s**
   she   leave**s**
   it   walk**s**
2 Verbs ending in -*s*, -*ss*, -*sh*, -*ch* add -*es*.
   he
   she   watch**es**
   it   wash**es**

❶ *go*, *have*, and *do* are irregular.
   he   does
   she   goes
   it   has

6.3 Adverbs of frequency

0%	40%	90%
never	sometimes	usually

These adverbs usually come before the verb.
   We **never** go out in the evening.
   He **usually** goes to work by taxi.
   She **sometimes** has a cup of coffee.

6.4 Present Simple *he / she / it*

Negative

She He	doesn't	go out in the evening. eat in a restaurant.

Questions with question words

What time Where When	does	he go to work? she have lunch?
		it leave?

Yes/No questions and short answers

Does he like football?	Yes, he does. No, he doesn't.
Does she speak English?	Yes, she does. No, she doesn't.

❶ Does he like tea?   Yes, he does.   NOT   ~~Yes, he likes.~~

7.1 Question words

Look at the question words and the answers.

What?	A hamburger.
When?	In the evening.
What time?	At 8.00.
Who?	Peter.
Where?	In Paris.
How?	By taxi.
How old?	16.
How many?	Two.
How much?	$2.
Why?	Because …

7.2 Object pronouns

Look at the subject and object pronouns, and the possessive adjectives.

Subject pronouns	Object pronouns	Possessive adjectives
I	me	my
you	you	your
he	him	his
she	her	her
it	it	its
we	us	our
they	them	their

7.3 *this/that*

We use *this* to refer to things near to us.

This is my son.   I like this sandwich.

We use *that* to refer to things that are not near to us.

That's my dog.   I don't like that car.

UNIT 8

8.1 *There is/There are*

Positive
There's a sofa in the living room.   (*There's = There is*)
There are two CD players in my house.

Question
Is there a TV in the kitchen?
Are there any magazines on the table?
How many CDs **are there**?

Negative
There isn't a TV.
There aren't any photos.

8.2 *any*

We use *any* in questions and negatives.
  Are there any books in the room?
  There are**n't any** CDs.

UNIT 9

9.1 *was/were*

Was and *were* are the past tense of *am/are/is.*

Present positive
I **am** happy.
You **are** a student.
He/She/It **is** in New York.
We **are** hot.
They **are** at work.

Past positive
I **was** happy yesterday.
You **were** a student in 1998.
He/She/It **was** in New York.
We **were** hot.
They **were** at work last week.

Negative

I He	wasn't	at home last weekend.
You They	weren't	at school yesterday.

Questions
Where **were you** yesterday?
Was she at school? Yes, **she was.**/No, **she wasn't.**

❶ We use *was/were* with *born*, not *am/is/are.*
  Where were you born?   Where ~~are~~ you born?
  He was born in Russia.   NOT   He ~~is~~ born in Russia.

9.2 Past Simple – irregular verbs

Many common verbs are irregular. See the list of irregular verbs on p142.

Present	**Past**
is/are	was/were
buy	bought
go	went
say	said
see	saw
take	took

UNIT 10

10.1 Past Simple positive

1 Regular verbs add *-ed* or *-d* in the Past Simple.

Present	**Past**
play	play**ed**
watch	watch**ed**
listen	listen**ed**
turn	turn**ed**
change	chang**ed**

2 Many common verbs are irregular.
  go   went
  see   saw
  have   had
  See the list on p142.

3 The form is the same for all persons.

I You He/She/It We They	listened to music. went to work. had lunch.

10.2 Past Simple questions and negatives

❶ Present *do/does* → Past *did*
  What time **does** he usually get up?
  What time **did** he get up yesterday?

Questions with question words

Where	did	I you he/she/it we they	go?

Negative

I We	didn't	go shopping. see my friends.

***Yes/no* questions and short answers**

Did they play football?	Yes, they did.
Did you have a good time?	No, I didn't.

UNIT 11

11.1 *can*

Positive

I You He/She/It We They	can	swim. drive. cook. run fast.

Negative

I You He/She/It We They	can't	draw. speak German. play golf.

Questions with question words

When		I go home?
What	can	you do?
How many languages		he speak?

Yes/No questions and short answers

Can you swim?	Yes, I can.
Can he play tennis?	No, he can't.

UNIT 12

12.1 *would like*

1 We use *would like* to ask for things.
    I'd like a magazine, please.   *'d = would*
    We'd like a cup of tea, please.

2 We use *would like* in questions to offer things.
    Would you **like** some cake?   Yes, please.
    Would you **like** a drink?   No, thank you.

❶ Would you like a cup of tea?   No, thank you. NOT ~~No, I wouldn't.~~

3 We can use *would like* with another verb.
    Would you like **to go out** tonight?
    What would you like **to do**?

12.2 *like* and *would like*

1 We use *like* and *like doing* to talk about things we always like.
    I **like** coffee. (= I always enjoy coffee.)
    She **likes** swimming in summer.
    What do you **like** doing at the weekend?

2 We use *would like* to talk about things we want *now*.
    I'd like a cup of tea. (= I want a cup of tea now.)
    She's hot. She**'d like** to go swimming.
    What **would** you **like** to do tonight?

12.3 *would like* and *want*

We use *would like*, not *want*, when we want to be polite.
    I'd like a coffee, please. NOT ~~I want a coffee.~~
    Would you like an ice-cream?

UNIT 13

13.1 Present Continuous

Positive

I	am	
He She It	is	working.
You We They	are	

13.2 Present Continuous

Negative

I	'm not	
He She It	isn't	working.
You We They	aren't	

Questions with question words

	am I	
What	are you are we are they	wearing?
	is he is she	

Yes/No **questions and short answers**

Are you wearing jeans?	Yes, I am. No, I'm not.
Is she reading a newspaper?	Yes, she is. No, she isn't.

13.3 Present Simple and Present Continuous

1 We use the Present Simple to talk about actions that are true for all time or a long time.
>   Hans **comes** from Germany.
>   I **love** you.
>   My father **works** in a bank.
>   I **get up** at 7.30 every day.
>   She **doesn't understand** French.

2 We use the Present Continuous to talk about actions that last a short time. The actions are happening *now*.
>   I usually wear jeans, but today I'**m wearing** a suit.
>   He'**s speaking** French to that man. He speaks French very well.
>   It'**s raining**.
>   They'**re swimming**.

UNIT 14

14.1 Present Continuous for future

1 See **Grammar Reference 13.1** and **13.2** for the forms of the Present Continuous – positive, negative, questions, and short answers.

2 We also use the Present Continuous to express **future plans**.
>   We're flying to Mexico **on Friday**.
>   I'm having lunch with Mary **on Tuesday**.
>   What are you doing **this weekend**?
>   I'm seeing the doctor **this week**.
>   We're having a party **next Saturday**. Can you come?

Word list

Here is a list of most of the new words in *New Headway Beginner*.

adj = adjective   *n* = noun   *pron* = pronoun
adv = adverb   *pl* = plural   *v* = verb
conj = conjunction   *prep* = preposition

UNIT 1

and *conj* /ænd/, /ənd/ _____
bag *n* /bæg/
book *n* /bʊk/
camera *n* /ˈkæmərə/ _____
car *n* /kɑː/ _____
computer *n* /kəmˈpjuːtə/ _____
fine *adj* /faɪn/ _____
hamburger *n* /ˈhæmbɜːgə/ _____
hello /həˈləʊ/
hi /haɪ/
house *n* /haʊs/ _____
How are you? /ˌhaʊ ə ˈjuː/ _____
my *adj* /maɪ/ _____
name *n* /neɪm/
number *n* /ˈnʌmbə/ _____
OK /əʊˈkeɪ/ _____
photograph *n* /ˈfəʊtəgrɑːf/ _____
sandwich *n* /ˈsænwɪdʒ/ _____
student *n* /ˈstjuːdənt/ _____
television *n* /ˈteləvɪʒn/ _____
thanks /θæŋks/
this /ðɪs/
very well /ˌveri ˈwel/ _____
what? /wɒt/ _____
your *adj* /jɔː/ _____

Numbers 1–10
one /wʌn/ _____
two /tuː/ _____
three /θriː/ _____
four /fɔː/ _____
five /faɪv/ _____
six /sɪks/ _____
seven /ˈsevn/ _____
eight /eɪt/ _____
nine /naɪn/ _____
ten /ten/ _____

UNIT 2

Australia *n* /ɒˈstreɪliə/
Brazil *n* /brəˈzɪl/
Canada *n* /ˈkænədə/
centre *n* /ˈsentə/
city *n* /ˈsɪti/
country *n* /ˈkʌntri/
doctor *n* /ˈdɒktə/
England *n* /ˈɪŋglənd/
France *n* /frɑːns/
from *prep* /frɒm/, /frəm/
her *adj* /hɜː/
his *adj* /hɪz/
hospital *n* /ˈhɒspɪtl/
in *prep* /ɪn/
it *pron* /ɪt/
Italy *n* /ˈɪtəli/
Japan *n* /dʒəˈpæn/
map *n* /mæp/
married *adj* /ˈmærɪd/
school *n* /skuːl/
Spain *n* /speɪn/
teacher *n* /ˈtiːtʃə/
the United States *n*
  /ðə juːˌnaɪtɪd ˈsteɪts/
too *adv* /tuː/
town *n* /taʊn/
where *adv* /weə/
world *n* /wɜːld/

Numbers 11–30
eleven /ɪˈlevn/
twelve /twelv/
thirteen /θɜːˈtiːn/ /ˈθɜːtiːn/
fourteen /fɔːˈtiːn/ /ˈfɔːtiːn/
fifteen /fɪfˈtiːn/ /ˈfɪftiːn/
sixteen /sɪksˈtiːn/ /ˈsɪkstiːn/
seventeen /sevnˈtiːn/ /ˈsevntiːn/
eighteen /eɪˈtiːn/ /ˈeɪtiːn/
nineteen /naɪnˈtiːn/ /ˈnaɪntiːn/
twenty /ˈtwenti/
twenty-one /ˌtwenti ˈwʌn/
twenty-two /ˌtwenti ˈtuː/
twenty-three /ˌtwenti ˈθriː/
twenty-four /ˌtwenti ˈfɔː/
twenty-five /ˌtwenti ˈfaɪv/
twenty-six /ˌtwenti ˈsɪks/
twenty-seven /ˌtwenti ˈsevn/
twenty-eight /ˌtwenti ˈeɪt/
twenty-nine /ˌtwenti ˈnaɪn/
thirty /ˈθɜːti/

UNIT 3

address *n* /əˈdres/
afternoon *n* /ɑːftəˈnuːn/
age *n* /eɪdʒ/
all right /ˌɔːl ˈraɪt/
American *adj* /əˈmerɪkən/
at *prep* /æt/, /ət/

businessman *n* /ˈbɪznɪsmən/
city *n* /ˈsɪti/
dictionary *n* /ˈdɪkʃənri/
evening *n* /ˈiːvnɪŋ/
good *adj* /gʊd/
goodbye /gʊdˈbaɪ/
great (= very good) *adj* /greɪt/
have a good journey /ˌhæv ə gʊd ˈdʒɜːni/
homework *n* /ˈhəʊmwɜːk/
hotel *n* /həʊˈtel/
how old? *adv* /ˌhaʊ ˈəʊld/
I don't know /aɪ ˌdəʊnt ˈnəʊ/
I don't understand /aɪ ˌdəʊnt ʌndəˈstænd/
job *n* /dʒɒb/
journey *n* /ˈdʒɜːni/
madam *n* /ˈmædəm/
morning *n* /ˈmɔːnɪŋ/
night *n* /naɪt/
nurse *n* /nɜːs/
of *prep* /ɒv/, /əv/
on tour /ˌɒn ˈtʊə/
page *n* /peɪdʒ/
pardon? /ˈpɑːdn/
personal information *n* /ˌpɜːsənl ɪnfəˈmeɪʃən/
phone number *n* /ˈfəʊn ˌnʌmbə/
police officer *n* /pəˈliːs ˌɒfɪsə/
pop group *n* /ˈpɒp ˌgruːp/
shop assistant *n* /ˈʃɒp əˌsɪstənt/
sir *n* /sɜː/
sleep well /ˌsliːp ˈwel/
sorry /ˈsɒri/
street *n* /striːt/
taxi driver *n* /ˈtæksi ˌdraɪvə/

UNIT 4

a lot of /ə ˈlɒt əv/
also *adv* /ˈɔːlsəʊ/
bank manager *n* /ˈbæŋk ˌmænɪdʒə/
beautiful *adj* /ˈbjuːtɪfl/
best *adj* /best/
big *adj* /bɪg/
both /bəʊθ/
brother *n* /ˈbrʌðə/
bus *n* /bʌs/
business card *n* /ˈbɪznɪs kɑːd/
but *conj* /bʌt/, /bət/
CD *n* /ˌsiː ˈdiː/
child *n* /tʃaɪld/
children *n* /ˈtʃɪldrən/
class *n* /klɑːs/
classroom *n* /ˈklɑːsrʊm/
college *n* /ˈkɒlɪdʒ/
country (not town) *n* /ˈkʌntri/
dad *n* /dæd/
daughter *n* /ˈdɔːtə/
director *n* /daɪˈrektə/
dog *n* /dɒg/
family *n* /ˈfæməli/
fan *n* /fæn/
farm *n* /fɑːm/
father *n* /ˈfɑːðə/
favourite *adj* /ˈfeɪvrɪt/
first name /ˈfɜːst ˌneɪm/
flat *n* /flæt/
friend *n* /frend/
funny *adj* /ˈfʌni/
Germany *n* /ˈdʒɜːməni/
girlfriend *n* /ˈgɜːlfrend/
happy *adj* /ˈhæpi/
have *v* /hæv/
have a good time /ˌhæv ə ˌgʊd ˈtaɪm/
husband *n* /ˈhʌzbənd/
manager *n* /ˈmænɪdʒə/
mother *n* /ˈmʌðə/
mum *n* /mʌm/
music *n* /ˈmjuːzɪk/
near *prep* /nɪə/
nice *adj* /naɪs/
office *n* /ˈɒfɪs/
our *adj* /ˈaʊə/
parent *n* /ˈpeərənt/
part-time *adj* /ˈpɑːt taɪm/
really *adv* /ˈriːəli/
sister *n* /ˈsɪstə/
small *adj* /smɔːl/
son *n* /sʌn/
spell *v* /spel/
surname *n* /ˈsɜːneɪm/
their *adj* /ðeə/
together *adv* /təˈgeðə/
university *n* /ˌjuːnɪˈvɜːsəti/
very *adv* /ˈveri/
who? /huː/
wife *n* /waɪf/

a little /ə 'lɪtl/ _____

actor n /'æktə/ _____

bar of chocolate n /ˌbɑːr əv 'tʃɒklət/ _____

be v /biː/ _____

beer n /bɪə/ _____

cheese n /tʃiːz/ _____

Chinese adj /tʃaɪ'niːz/ _____

coffee n /'kɒfi/ _____

drama student n /'drɑːmə ˌstjuːdənt/ _____

drink v, n /drɪŋk/ _____

eat v /iːt/ _____

food n /fuːd/ _____

football n /'fʊtbɔːl/ _____

French adj /frentʃ/ _____

German adj /'dʒɜːmən/ _____

how many? /ˌhaʊ 'meni/ _____

how much? /ˌhaʊ 'mʌtʃ/ _____

ice-cream n /'aɪs kriːm/ _____

identity n /aɪ'dentɪti/ _____

Italian adj /ɪ'tæliən/ _____

Japanese adj /dʒæpə'niːz/ _____

language n /'læŋgwɪdʒ/ _____

life n /laɪf/ _____

like v /laɪk/ _____

live v /lɪv/ _____

love v /lʌv/ _____

Mexico n /'meksɪkəʊ/ _____

mobile phone n /ˌməʊbaɪl 'fəʊn/ _____

nationality n /næʃə'næləti/ _____

now adv /naʊ/ _____

orange n /'ɒrɪndʒ/ _____

party n /'pɑːti/ _____

pizza n /'piːtsə/ _____

place n /pleɪs/ _____

play v /pleɪ/ _____

Portugal n /'pɔːtʃʊgl/ _____

Portuguese adj /pɔːtʃʊ'giːz/ _____

pound n /paʊnd/ _____

price n /praɪs/ _____

radio n /'reɪdiəʊ/ _____

restaurant n /'restrɒnt/ _____

Scotland n /'skɒtlənd/ _____

skiing n /'skiːɪŋ/ _____

Spanish adj /'spænɪʃ/ _____

speak v /spiːk/ _____

sport n /spɔːt/ _____

swimming n /'swɪmɪŋ/ _____

Switzerland n /'swɪtsələnd/ _____

tea n /tiː/ _____

tennis n /'tenɪs/ _____

think v /θɪŋk/ _____

waiter n /'weɪtə/ _____

want v /wɒnt/ _____

wine n /waɪn/ _____

work v /wɜːk/ _____

Numbers 40–100

forty /'fɔːti/ _____

fifty /'fɪfti/ _____

sixty /'sɪksti/ _____

seventy /'sevnti/ _____

eighty /'eɪti/ _____

ninety /'naɪnti/ _____

one hundred /ˌwʌn 'hʌndrəd/ _____

artist *n* /ˈɑːtɪst/
at home *adv* /ət ˈhəʊm/

breakfast *n* /ˈbrekfəst/
buy *v* /baɪ/
by bus /ˌbaɪ ˈbʌs/
by taxi /ˌbaɪ ˈtæksi/

clock *n* /klɒk/
cook *v* /kʊk/

day *n* /deɪ/
dinner *n* /ˈdɪnə/
director *n* /dəˈrektə, dɪ-, daɪ-/

early *adj* /ˈɜːli/   *late*

get home *v* /ˌget ˈhəʊm/
get up *v* /ˌget ˈʌp/
glass *n* /glɑːs/
go *v* /gəʊ/
go for a walk /ˌgəʊ fər ə ˈwɔːk/
go out /ˌgəʊ ˈaʊt/
go shopping /ˌgəʊ ˈʃɒpɪŋ/
go to bed /ˌgəʊ tə ˈbed/
grandfather *n* /ˈgrænfɑːðə/

have a shower /ˌhæv ə ˈʃaʊə/
have breakfast /ˌhæv ˈbrekfəst/
have lunch /ˌhæv ˈlʌntʃ/

late *adj* /leɪt/
leave school/home /ˌliːv ˈskuːl,
    ˈhəʊm/

listen to music /ˌlɪsn tə ˈmjuːzɪk/

millionaire *n* /mɪljəˈneə/

never *adv* /ˈnevə/
nine o'clock /ˌnaɪn əˈklɒk/

paint *v* /peɪnt/
play the piano /ˌpleɪ ðə piˈænəʊ/

site on the Internet /ˌsaɪt ɒn ði
    ˈɪntənet/
sometimes *adv* /ˈsʌmtaɪmz/
stay at home /ˌsteɪ ət ˈhəʊm/
studio *n* /ˈstjuːdiəʊ/

thank you very much /ˌθæŋk juː
    ˌveri ˈmʌtʃ/
time *n* /taɪm/
toast *n* /təʊst/
today *n* /təˈdeɪ/
tomorrow *n* /təˈmɒrəʊ/

until *prep* /ʌnˈtɪl/
usually *adv* /ˈjuːʒəli/

walk to school /ˌwɔːk tə ˈskuːl/
watch TV /ˌwɒtʃ tiː ˈviː/
week *n* /wiːk/
weekend *n* /wiːkˈend/
what time is it? /wɒt ˈtaɪm ɪz ɪt/
when? /wen/

beach *n* /biːtʃ/ _____

because *conj* /bɪˈkɒz/ _____

boy *n* /bɔɪ/ _____

boyfriend *n* /ˈbɔɪfrend/ _____

building *n* /ˈbɪldɪŋ/ _____

café *n* /ˈkæfeɪ/ _____

capital city *n* /ˌkæpɪtl ˈsɪti/ _____

cat *n* /kæt/ _____

champagne *n* /ʃæmˈpeɪn/ _____

change a traveller's cheque
  /ˌtʃeɪndʒ ə ˌtrævələz ˈtʃek/ _____

changing room *n* /ˈtʃeɪndʒɪŋ
  ˌruːm/ _____

cheap *adj* /tʃiːp/ _____

chocolate *n* /ˈtʃɒklət/ _____

clothes shop *n* /ˈkləʊðz ˌʃɒp/ _____

cold *adj* /kəʊld/ _____

comfortable *adj* /ˈkʌmftəbl/ _____

delicious *adj* /dɪˈlɪʃəs/ _____

email *n* /ˈiːmeɪl/ _____

every /ˈevri/ _____

expensive *adj* /ɪkˈspensɪv/ _____

famous *adj* /ˈfeɪməs/ _____

fantastic *adj* /fænˈtæstɪk/ _____

film star *n* /ˈfɪlm stɑː/ _____

first /fɜːst/ _____

floor *n* /flɔː/ _____

friendly *adj* /ˈfrendli/ _____

girl *n* /gɜːl/ _____

give *v* /gɪv/ _____

hate *v* /heɪt/ _____

help *v* /help/ _____

here *adv* /hɪə/ _____

homework *n* /ˈhəʊmwɜːk/ _____

horrible *adj* /ˈhɒrəbl/ _____

hot *adj* /hɒt/ _____

international *adj* /ɪntəˈnæʃnəl/ _____

Internet *n* /ˈɪntənet/ _____

Irish *adj* /ˈaɪrɪʃ/ _____

jacket *n* /ˈdʒækɪt/ _____

journalist *n* /ˈdʒɜːnəlɪst/ _____

lovely *adj* /ˈlʌvli/ _____

marry *v* /ˈmæri/ _____

money *n* /ˈmʌni/ _____

movies *n pl* /ˈmuːvɪz/ _____

new *adj* /njuː/ _____

of course /əv ˈkɔːs/ _____

postcard *n* /ˈpəʊskɑːd/ _____

present (for someone's birthday)
  n /ˈprezənt/ _____

president *n* /ˈprezɪdənt/ _____

pyramid *n* /ˈpɪrəmɪd/ _____

railway station *n* /ˈreɪlweɪ ˌsteɪʃn/ _____

return ticket *n* /rɪˌtɜːn ˈtɪkɪt/ _____

see you soon /ˌsiː juː ˈsuːn/ _____

send *v* /send/ _____

single ticket *n* /ˈsɪŋgl ˈtɪkɪt/ _____

teach *v* /tiːtʃ/ _____

that /ðæt/ _____

try on a jumper /ˌtraɪ ɒn ə
  ˈdʒʌmpə/ _____

T-shirt *n* /ˈtiː ʃɜːt/ _____

vacation *n* /veɪˈkeɪʃn/ _____

very much /ˌveri ˈmʌtʃ/ _____

visit *v* /ˈvɪzɪt/ _____

weather *n* /ˈweðə/ _____

wedding *n* /ˈwedɪŋ/ _____

wet *adj* /wet/ _____

White House *n* /ˈwaɪt ˌhaʊs/ _____

why? /waɪ/ _____

with *prep* /wɪð/ _____

a few /ə 'fju:/ _____

armchair n /'ɑ:mtʃeə/ _____

autumn n /'ɔ:təm/ _____

bar n /bɑ:/ _____

bathroom n /'bɑ:θrʊm/ _____

bed n /bed/ _____

bedroom n /'bedrʊm/ _____

CD player n /si: 'di: ˌpleɪə/ _____

chemist n /'kemɪst/ _____

church n /tʃɜ:tʃ/ _____

cinema n /'sɪnəmə/ _____

club n /klʌb/ _____

company n /'kʌmpəni/ _____

cooker n /'kʊkə/ _____

credit card n /'kredɪt ˌkɑ:d/ _____

different adj /'dɪfrənt/ _____

dining room n /'daɪnɪŋ rʊm/ _____

drawer n /'drɔ:/ _____

engineer n /endʒə'nɪə/ _____

everything pron /'evriθɪŋ/ _____

fast adv /fɑ:st/ _____

ferry n /'feri/ _____

fresh adj /freʃ/ _____

garden n /'gɑ:dn/ _____

go running n /gəʊ 'rʌnɪŋ/ _____

go straight on /ˌgəʊ streɪt 'ɒn/ _____

harbour n /'hɑ:bə/ _____

key n /ki:/ _____

kitchen n /'kɪtʃən/ _____

lamp n /læmp/ _____

Lebanese adj /lebə'ni:z/ _____

living room n /'lɪvɪŋ ˌrʊm/ _____

magazine n /mægə'zi:n/ _____

market n /'mɑ:kɪt/ _____

newsagent n /'nju:zeɪdʒənt/ _____

next to prep /'neks tu:/, /tə/ _____

night-life n /'naɪt laɪf/ _____

on prep /ɒn/ _____

opera n /'ɒprə/ _____

pen n /pen/ _____

picture n /'pɪktʃə/ _____

post office n /'pəʊst ˌɒfɪs/ _____

room n /ru:m/ _____

run v /rʌn/ _____

sailing n /'seɪlɪŋ/ _____

seafood n /'si:fu:d/ _____

shoe n /ʃu:/ _____

shower n /'ʃaʊə/ _____

sign n /saɪn/ _____

slow adj /sləʊ/ _____

sofa n /'səʊfə/ _____

spring n /sprɪŋ/ _____

stay v /steɪ/ _____

summer n /'sʌmə/ _____

supermarket n /'su:pəmɑ:kɪt/ _____

surfing n /'sɜ:fɪŋ/ _____

table n /'teɪbl/ _____

Thai adj /taɪ/ _____

theatre n /'θɪətə/ _____

toilet n /'tɔɪlət/ _____

train n /treɪn/ _____

travel v /'trævl/ _____

Turkish adj /'tɜ:kɪʃ/ _____

turn left/right /ˌtɜ:n 'left, 'raɪt/ _____

under prep /'ʌndə/ _____

video recorder n /'vɪdiəʊ rɪˌkɔ:də/ _____

Vietnamese adj /vietnə'mi:z/ _____

walk n /wɔ:k/ _____

wall n /wɔ:l/ _____

way (to see Sydney) /weɪ/ _____

windsurfing n /'wɪndsɜ:fɪŋ/ _____

wonderful adj /wʌndəfl/ _____

birthday *n* /'bɜ:θdeɪ/ _____

calendar *n* /'kælɪndə/ _____

dirty *adj* /'dɜ:ti/ _____

expert *n* /'ekspɜ:t/ _____

Holland *n* /'hɒlənd/ _____

India /'ɪndɪə/ _____

market *n* /'mɑ:kɪt/ _____

million /'mɪljən/ _____

musician *n* /mju:'zɪʃn/ _____

painter *n* /'peɪntə/ _____

painting *n* /'peɪntɪŋ/ _____

politician *n* /ˌpɒlə'tɪʃn/ _____

princess *n* /prɪn'ses/ _____

racing driver *n* /'reɪsɪŋ ˌdraɪvə/ _____

say *v* /seɪ/ _____

scientist *n* /'saɪəntɪst/ _____

see *v* /si:/ _____

sell *v* /sel/ _____

singer *n* /'sɪŋə/ _____

so /səʊ/ _____

take *v* /teɪk/ _____

thousand /'θaʊzənd/ _____

upset *adj* /ʌp'set/ _____

Virgin Mary /ˌvɜ:dʒɪn 'meəri/ _____

was/were born /ˌwɒz, wəz, wɜ:, wə 'bɔ:n/ _____

worth *adj* /wɜ:θ/ _____

writer *n* /'raɪtə/ _____

year *n* /jɪə/ _____

yesterday *adv* /'jestədeɪ/ _____

Months of the year

January /'dʒænʊəri/ _____

February /'februəri/ _____

March /mɑ:tʃ/ _____

April /'eɪprəl/ _____

May /meɪ/ _____

June /dʒu:n/ _____

July /dʒʊ'laɪ/ _____

August /'ɔ:gəst/ _____

September /sep'tembə/ _____

October /ɒk'təʊbə/ _____

November /nəʊ'vembə/ _____

December /dɪ'sembə/ _____

a bit /ə 'bɪt/ _____

application form *n* /æplɪ'keɪʃn fɔ:m/ _____

athletics *n* /æθ'letɪks/ _____

baseball *n* /'beɪsbɔ:l/ _____

bread *n* /bred/ _____

cards *n pl* /kɑ:dz/ _____

chalet *n* /'ʃæleɪ/ _____

chip *n* /tʃɪp/ _____

date *n* /deɪt/ _____

date of birth *n* /deɪt əv 'bɜ:θ/ _____

egg *n* /eg/ _____

fill in *v* /fɪl ɪn/ _____

film *n* /fɪlm/ _____

fitness training *n* /'fɪtnəs ˌtreɪnɪŋ/ _____

full name /fʊl neɪm/ _____

fun *n* /fʌn/ _____

go dancing /gəʊ 'dɑ:nsɪŋ/ _____

golf *n* /gɒlf/ _____

have a nice weekend /ˌhæv ə ˌnaɪs wi:k'end/ _____

housework *n* /'haʊswɜ:k/ _____

ice-hockey *n* /'aɪs ˌhɒki/ _____

ice-skating *n* /'aɪs ˌskeɪtɪŋ/ _____

join *v* /dʒɔɪn/ _____

last (year) /lɑ:st/ _____

lazy *adj* /'leɪzi/ _____

lovely *adj* /'lʌvli/ _____

meal *n* /mi:l/ _____

midnight *n* /'mɪdnaɪt/ _____

newspaper *n* /'nju:speɪpə/ _____

orange juice *n* /'ɒrɪndʒ ˌdʒu:s/ _____

own *adj* /əʊn/ _____

postcode *n* /'pəʊstkəʊd/ _____

salad *n* /'sæləd/ _____

season *n* /'si:zn/ _____

shopping *n* /'ʃɒpɪŋ/ _____

signature *n* /'sɪgnətʃə/ _____

sit *v* /sɪt/ _____

soup *n* /su:p/ _____

sports centre *n* /'spɔ:ts sentə/ _____

steak *n* /steɪk/ _____

sun *n* /sʌn/ _____

wet *adj* /wet/ _____

winter *n* /'wɪntə/ _____

yesterday afternoon /ˌjestədeɪ ɑ:ftə'nu:n/ _____

yesterday evening /ˌjestədeɪ 'i:vnɪŋ/ _____

yesterday morning /ˌjestədeɪ 'mɔ:nɪŋ/ _____

UNIT 11

about /ə'baʊt/ _____
again _adv_ /ə'gen/ _____
airport _n_ /'eəpɔ:t/ _____
all /ɔ:l/ _____
all over the world /,ɔ:l ,əʊvə ðə
  'wɜ:ld/ _____
anyway _adv_ /'eniweɪ/ _____
architect _n_ /'ɑ:kitekt/ _____
athlete _n_ /'æθli:t/ _____
book _v_ /bʊk/ _____
borrow _v_ /'bɒrəʊ/ _____
bring _v_ /brɪŋ/ _____
cake _n_ /keɪk/ _____
can _v_ /kæn/, /kən/ _____
chat _v_ /tʃæt/ _____
check _v_ /tʃek/ _____
chess _n_ /tʃes/ _____
cold drink /,kəʊld 'drɪŋk/ _____
communicate _v_ /kə'mju:nɪkeɪt/ _____
company _n_ /'kʌmpəni/ _____
computer games _n pl_ /kəm'pju:tə
  ,geɪmz/ _____
department of defense (US)
  /dɪ,pɑ:tmənt əv dɪ'fens/ _____
draw _v_ /drɔ:/ _____
drive _v_ /draɪv/ _____
endless _adj_ /'endləs/ _____
excuse me /ɪk'skju:z mi:/ _____
find _v_ /faɪnd/ _____
flowers _n pl_ /'flaʊəz/ _____
forecast _n_ /'fɔ:kɑ:st/ _____
forget _v_ /fə'get/ _____
guitar _n_ /gɪ'tɑ:/ _____
history _n_ /'hɪstri/ _____
horse _n_ /hɔ:s/ _____
Internet (the Net) _n_ /'ɪntənet
  (ðə 'net)/ _____
interpreter _n_ /ɪn'tɜ:prɪtə/ _____
it doesn't matter /ɪt ,dʌznt
  'mætə/ _____
list _n_ /lɪst/ _____
lost /lɒst/ _____
make _v_ /meɪk/ _____
make possible /,meɪk 'pɒsəbl/ _____
many more /,meni 'mɔ:/ _____
mean _v_ /mi:n/ _____
military _adj_ /'mɪlətri/ _____
miss (the bus) _v_ /mɪs (ðə bʌs)/ _____
network _n_ /'netwɜ:k/ _____
next time /'neks ,taɪm/ _____
north /nɔ:θ/ _____
often /'ɒfn/ _____
on business /,ɒn 'bɪznəs/ _____
other /'ʌðə/ _____
partner _n_ /'pɑ:tnə/ _____
passport _n_ /'pɑ:spɔ:t/ _____
plane (aeroplane) _n_ /pleɪn
  ('eərəpleɪn)/ _____
problem _n_ /'prɒbləm/ _____
push _v_ /pʊʃ/ _____
put _v_ /pʊt/ _____
ride _v_ /raɪd/ _____

run _v_ /rʌn/ _____
Russian _adj_ /'rʌʃn/ _____
slowly _adv_ /'sləʊli/ _____
song _n_ /sɒŋ/ _____
start _v_ /stɑ:t/ _____
subject _n_ /'sʌbdʒɪkt/ _____
swim _v_ /swɪm/ _____
tell me the time /,tel mi: ðə 'taɪm/ _____
terrible _adj_ /'terəbl/ _____
thing _n_ /θɪŋ/ _____
ticket machine _n_ /'tɪkɪt mə,ʃi:n/ _____
tractor _n_ /'træktə/ _____
use _v_ /ju:z/ _____
wait a minute /,weɪt ə 'mɪnɪt/ _____
web _n_ /web/ _____
website _n_ /'websaɪt/ _____
worldwide _adv, adj_ /wɜ:ld'waɪd/ _____

apple pie *n* /ˌæpl ˈpaɪ/

bacon *n* /ˈbeɪkn/

(pay a) bill *n* /bɪl/

birthday card *n* /ˈbɜːθdeɪ ˌkɑːd/

black coffee *n* /ˌblæk ˈkɒfi/

bottle *n* /ˈbɒtl/

burger *n* /ˈbɜːgə/

carrots *n pl* /ˈkærəts/

certainly *adv* /ˈsɜːtənli/

change *n* /tʃeɪndʒ/

chicken *n* /ˈtʃɪkɪn/

cocktail *n* /ˈkɒkteɪl/

cream *n* /kriːm/

cup *n* /kʌp/

dessert *n* /dɪˈzɜːt/

die *v* /daɪ/

electricity bill *n* /ɪlekˈtrɪsəti ˌbɪl/

feel at home /ˌfiːl ət ˈhəʊm/

film (for my camera) *n* /fɪlm/

fish *n* /fɪʃ/

flavour *n* /ˈfleɪvə/

fries (= chips) *n pl* /fraɪz/

fruit *n* /fruːt/

generation *n* /dʒenəˈreɪʃn/

get (= buy) *v* /get/

get (= fetch) *v* /get/

granddaughter *n* /ˈgrændɔːtə/

grandma *n* /ˈgrænmɑː/

hairdresser *n* /ˈheədresə/

I'm just looking /ˌaɪm ˌdʒʌst ˈlʊkɪŋ/

Indian *adj* /ˈɪndiən/

jumper *n* /ˈdʒʌmpə/

junk food *n* /ˈdʒʌŋk ˌfuːd/

kilo *n* /ˈkiːləʊ/

lettuce *n* /ˈletɪs/

main course *n* /ˈmeɪn ˌkɔːs/

meat *n* /miːt/

menu *n* /ˈmenjuː/

mineral water *n* /ˈmɪnərəl ˌwɔːtə/

mixed salad *n* /ˌmɪkst ˈsæləd/

oldest *adj* /ˈəʊldɪst/

order *v* /ˈɔːdə/

pair of jeans *n* /ˌpeər əv ˈdʒiːnz/

peas *n pl* /piːz/

person *n* /ˈpɜːsn/

phone card *n* /ˈfəʊn ˌkɑːd/

popcorn *n* /ˈpɒpkɔːn/

potato *n* /pəˈteɪtəʊ/

program *n* /ˈprəʊgræm/

red *adj* /red/

roast (chicken) *adj* /rəʊst/

single *n* /ˈsɪŋgl/

size *n* /saɪz/

small/medium/large *adj* /smɔːl/, /ˈmiːdiəm/, /lɑːdʒ/

stamp *n* /stæmp/

still/sparkling water /stɪl/, /ˌspɑːklɪŋ ˈwɔːtə/

sure *adj* /ʃʊə/

test *n* /test/

tomato *n* /təˈmɑːtəʊ/

tonight *adv* /təˈnaɪt/

try *v* /traɪ/

try on /ˌtraɪ ˈɒn/

vanilla *n* /vəˈnɪlə/

vegetable *n* /ˈvedʒtəbl/

white coffee *n* /ˌwaɪt ˈkɒfi/

you bet! /juː ˈbet/

UNIT 13

anything *pron* /ˈeniθɪŋ/

barbeque *n* /ˈbɑːbɪkjuː/

boot *n* /buːt/

Christmas Day *n* /ˌkrɪsməs ˈdeɪ/

coat *n* /kəʊt/

dress *n* /dres/

during *prep* /ˈdjʊərɪŋ/

enjoy *v* /ɪnˈdʒɔɪ/

eye *n* /aɪ/

fair *adj* /feə/

fashion show *n* /ˈfæʃən ˌʃəʊ/

get married /ˌget ˈmærɪd/

get ready /ˌget ˈredi/

hair *n* /heə/

hat *n* /hæt/

hungry *adj* /ˈhʌŋgri/

interview *n* /ˈɪntəvjuː/

jacket *n* /ˈdʒækɪt/

listeners *n pl* /ˈlɪsnəz/

love story *n* /ˈlʌv ˌstɔːri/

meet *v* /miːt/

model *n* /ˈmɒdl/

pack bags /ˌpæk ˈbægz/

rain *v* /reɪn/

read *v* /riːd/

sandal *n* /ˈsændl/

shirt *n* /ʃɜːt/

shoe *n* /ʃuː/

short *adj* /ʃɔːt/

shorts *n pl* /ʃɔːts/

skirt *n* /skɜːt/

sock *n* /sɒk/

special *adj* /ˈspeʃl/

swimsuit *n* /ˈswɪmsuːt/

talk *v* /tɔːk/

the news *n* /ðə ˈnjuːz/

thirsty *adj* /ˈθɜːsti/

tie *n* /taɪ/

tired *adj* /ˈtaɪəd/

trainers *n pl* /ˈtreɪnəz/

trousers *n pl* /ˈtraʊzəz/

wash *v* /wɒʃ/

wear *v* /weə/

what's the matter? /ˌwɒts ðə ˈmætə/

Colours

black /blæk/

blue /bluː/

brown /braʊn/

green /griːn/

grey /greɪ/

red /red/

yellow /ˈjeləʊ/

white /waɪt/

 UNIT 14

adult *n* /ˈædʌlt/

amazing *adj* /əˈmeɪzɪŋ/

Arctic Circle *n* /ˌɑːktɪk ˈsɜːkl/

arrive *v* /əˈraɪv/

bicycle *n* /ˈbaɪsɪkl/

bus tour *n* /ˈbʌs ˌtʊə/

busy *adj* /ˈbɪzi/

catch a plane /ˌkætʃ ə ˈpleɪn/

collect *v* /kəˈlekt/

cost *v* /kɒst/

diary *n* /ˈdaɪəri/

excited *adj* /ɪkˈsaɪtɪd/

flight *n* /flaɪt/

fly *v* /flaɪ/

future *n* /ˈfjuːtʃə/

go jogging /ˌgəʊ ˈdʒɒgɪŋ/

go sightseeing /ˌgəʊ ˈsaɪtsiːɪŋ/

hostel *n* /ˈhɒstl/

how long? /ˌhaʊ ˈlɒŋ/

it's time to go /ɪts ˌtaɪm tə ˈgəʊ/

last month /ˌlɑːst ˈmʌnθ/

lucky *adj* /ˈlʌki/

market *n* /ˈmɑːkɪt/

motorbike *n* /ˈməʊtəbaɪk/

museum *n* /mjuːˈziːəm/

New Zealand *n* /ˌnjuː ˈziːlənd/

plan *n* /plæn/

rucksack *n* /ˈrʌksæk/

ship *n* /ʃɪp/

still *adv* /stɪl/

suitcase *n* /ˈsuːtkeɪs/

the next one /ðə ˈnekst ˌwʌn/

ticket *n* /ˈtɪkɪt/

travel agent *n* /ˈtrævəl ˌeɪdʒənt/

uncle *n* /ˈʌŋkl/

(the) Underground *n* /(ðɪ) ˈʌndəgraʊnd/

via *prep* /ˈvaɪə/

youth hostel *n* /ˈjuːθ ˌhɒstl/

Pairwork activities

Cities and countries

2 Student B
Ask your partner questions and write the answers to complete the information.

> What's her name?

> Where's she from?

1
Her name's _____
She's from _____

2
Her name's Carole.
She's from Oxford.

3
His name's _____
He's from Pari_____

4
Her name's Paula.
She's from Rio de Janeiro.

5
His name's _____
He's from Sydn_____

6
Her name's Elena.
She's from Milan.

7
His name's _____
He's from Boston

8
His name's Carlos.
He's from Barcelona.

Different rooms

3 Student B

Look at the picture of a room. Your
partner has a different room. Talk about
your pictures to find six differences.

> In my picture, there's a ...

> In my picture, there isn't a ...

> Is there a ... ?

> No, there isn't.

UNIT 14 *p107*

Listening and speaking

3 Student A

Read about Rachel and Lara's holiday plans. Answer
questions about Rachel and Lara. Ask your partner
questions about Didier. Complete the chart.

> Where is Didier going?

> Why is he going there?

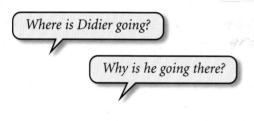

	Rachel + Lara	Didier
Where / go?	Whangaparada, New Zealand	
Why / go?	to visit their uncle	
When / leave?	22 December	
How / travel?	by plane and car	
Where / stay?	their uncle's house	
How long / stay?	three weeks	

Listening and speaking

3 Student B

Read about Didier's holiday plans. Answer questions about Didier. Ask your partner questions about Rachel and Lara. Complete the chart.

> *Where are Rachel and Lara going?*

> *Why are they going there?*

	Rachel + Lara	Didier
Where / go?		Scotland
Why / go?		to go walking
When / leave?		next Saturday
How / travel?		by train from Paris to Edinburgh, then by bus
Where / stay?		in youth hostels
How long / stay?		a week

Phonetic symbols

Consonants

1	/p/	as in	**pen** /pen/
2	/b/	as in	**big** /bɪg/
3	/t/	as in	**tea** /tiː/
4	/d/	as in	**do** /duː/
5	/k/	as in	**cat** /kæt/
6	/g/	as in	**go** /gəʊ/
7	/f/	as in	**four** /fɔː/
8	/v/	as in	**very** /'veri/
9	/s/	as in	**son** /sʌn/
10	/z/	as in	**zoo** /zuː/
11	/l/	as in	**live** /lɪv/
12	/m/	as in	**my** /maɪ/
13	/n/	as in	**now** /naʊ/
14	/h/	as in	**happy** /'hæpi/
15	/r/	as in	**red** /red/
16	/j/	as in	**yes** /jes/
17	/w/	as in	**want** /wɒnt/
18	/θ/	as in	**thanks** /θæŋks/
19	/ð/	as in	**the** /ðə/
20	/ʃ/	as in	**she** /ʃiː/
21	/ʒ/	as in	**television** /'telɪvɪʒn/
22	/tʃ/	as in	**child** /tʃaɪld/
23	/dʒ/	as in	**German** /'dʒɜːmən/
24	/ŋ/	as in	**English** /'ɪŋglɪʃ/

Vowels

25	/iː/	as in	**see** /siː/
26	/ɪ/	as in	**his** /hɪz/
27	/i/	as in	**twenty** /'twenti/
28	/e/	as in	**ten** /ten/
29	/æ/	as in	**bag** /bæg/
30	/ɑː/	as in	**father** /'fɑːðə/
31	/ɒ/	as in	**hot** /hɒt/
32	/ɔː/	as in	**morning** /'mɔːnɪŋ/
33	/ʊ/	as in	**football** /'fʊtbɔːl/
34	/uː/	as in	**you** /juː/
35	/ʌ/	as in	**sun** /sʌn/
36	/ɜː/	as in	**learn** /lɜːn/
37	/ə/	as in	**letter** /'letə/

Diphthongs (two vowels together)

38	/eɪ/	as in	**name** /neɪm/
39	/əʊ/	as in	**no** /nəʊ/
40	/aɪ/	as in	**my** /maɪ/
41	/aʊ/	as in	**how** /haʊ/
42	/ɔɪ/	as in	**boy** /bɔɪ/
43	/ɪə/	as in	**hear** /hɪə/
44	/eə/	as in	**where** /weə/
45	/ʊə/	as in	**tour** /tʊə/

Irregular verbs

Base form	Past Simple
be	was/were
bring	brought
buy	bought
can	could
come	came
cost	cost
do	did
draw	drew
drink	drank
drive	drove
eat	ate
feel	felt
find	found
fly	flew
forget	forgot
get	got
give	gave
go	went
have	had
know	knew
leave	left
make	made
mean	meant
meet	met
pay	paid
put	put
read /ri:d/	read /red/
ride	rode
run	ran
say	said
see	saw
sell	sold
send	sent
sit	sat
speak	spoke
take	took
teach	taught
think	thought
understand	understood
wear	wore

OXFORD
UNIVERSITY PRESS

Great Clarendon Street, Oxford OX2 6DP

Oxford University Press is a department of the University of Oxford.

It furthers the University's objective of excellence in research, scholarship, and education by publishing worldwide in

Oxford New York

Auckland Bangkok Buenos Aires Cape Town Chennai Dar es Salaam Delhi Hong Kong Istanbul Karachi Kolkata Kuala Lumpur Madrid Melbourne Mexico City Mumbai Nairobi São Paulo Shanghai Taipei Tokyo Toronto

Oxford and Oxford English are registered trade marks of Oxford University Press in the UK and in certain other countries

© Oxford University Press 2000

Database right Oxford University Press (maker)

First published 2002
Seventh impression 2004

ISBN 0 19 437631 1

Printed and bound in Hong Kong

Acknowledgements

The authors and publisher are grateful to those who have given permission to reproduce the following extracts and adaptations of copyright material:

p108 'Mini happy returns' by Bill Mouland. Appeared in the *Daily Mail* 27 October 1999. Reproduced by permission of Daily Mail/Solo Syndication.

Illustrations by:

Adrian Barclay pp63, 97; Lisa Berkshire pp18, 110; Mark Blade/New Division p11; Matthew Booth/The Art Market p56; Matthew Cooper/Debut Art p30; Ben Croft/ The Art Collection pp96, 97; Paul Daviz pp6, 86, 87, 99, 103, 124; Graham Humphries/The Art Market p46; Marie-Hélène Jeeves pp33, 52, 83, 90; Di Mainstone/ CIA pp41, 59, 139; Kate Miller/CIA pp50, 70; Gavin Reece/New Division pp38, 74; Nicola Slater/Thorogood Agency pp23, 68, 69; Sparky p13; Technical Graphics Dept, OUP p109

Comm... ...7, 8, 9, 10 (car, camera), 12, 15 (...room), 22, 23, 34, 37 (camera, dictionary, wine), 39 (bag), 40, 42, 43, 49, 54 (café, shop, station, bank), 57, 58, 72, 73, 80 (Josh), 81 (Mabel, Josh), 95, 98, 101 (Becca), 104, 105; Haddon Davies p6; Julie Fisher pp16, 93; Mark Mason pp10 (bag, book), 29, 37 (coffee, bag, oranges), 39 (camera, dictionary), 89, 104 (diary), 110 (map)

We would also like to thank the following for permission to reproduce photographs:

Action-Plus p76 (G Kirk/tennis, sailing), (N Tingle/ football, skiing), (M Hewitt/golf), (T Henshaw/skating), (M King/dancing); AKG London pp64 (Curie), 66 (Monroe, Beethoven); Alamy.com p16 (M Del Grosso/ NY background); Anthony Blake Photo Library pp10 (RDL/sandwich), 32 (G Kirk/Chinese food), (T Hill/tea), (PFT Associates/Coke), 37 (Maximilian/beer), 39 (T Hill/ sandwich), 92 (Maximilian/cheese and mineral water), (M Brigdale/soup), (T Hill/chips), 10 (Courtesy of Apple); The Bridgeman Art Library pp64 (Biblioteca Reale, Turin, Italy/Leonardo da Vinci Self-Portrait, c.1513), 66 (British Library, London/Shakespeare), (Musée d'Orsay/Van Gogh Self-Portrait, 1889); Bruce Coleman Collection p27 (H Reinhard/dogs); Bubbles Photo Library pp13 (V Bonomo/Marie), (J Woodcock/Sergio & Kim), 90 (J Woodcock/Suzanne); Christopher Moore Ltd p102; Christine Osborne Pictures pp36 (1), 61 (ferry); Collections pp24 (R Davis/school), 45 (B West/cottage), 53 (J Nieman/musicians); Corbis pp14 and 138 (R Cummins/ Boston), 45 (D Degnan/piano), 67 (Bettmann/Ghandi), (S Carmona/Senna), 85 (K Fleming/two women in Internet café); Courtesy of the Edinburgh Tourist Board p111 (map); Elizabeth Whiting Associates p24 (house); Courtesy of the Fairmont Banff Springs p106 (hotel and skiing); Frank Spooner Pictures p67 (I Jones/Gamma/ Princess Diana); GettyOne Image Bank pp14 and 138 (W Bokelberg/woman from Milan), 45 (B Mitchell/ walking the dog), 101 (R Lockyer/Australia); GettyOne Stone pp9 (L Adamski Peek/tennis players), 13 (G Butera/ Jack), (J McLoughlin/Sonia), 14 and 138 (C Ehlers/ Tokyo), (J Lawrence/Oxford), (D Smetzer/girl from Rio), (J Truchet/Rio), 15 and 138 (P Correz/man from Barcelona), (F Hernholdt/Barcelona), (C Ehlers/Sydney), 15 (K Brofsky/business woman shaking hands), 17 (S Layda/flat iron building NY), 21 (A Weinbrecht/Diana), 22 (P Lee Harvey/4 x 4 pop group), 24 (B Ayres/Sally's family), 28 (D Jaffe/Andy & Carrie), 29 (D Day/parents), 29 (J S Simon/sisters), 32 (D Young Wolff/football), (L Evans/pizza), 36 (J Strachan/2), (J Darell/3), 37 (A Buckingham/car), 39 (Davies & Starr/beer), (C Rosenfeld/chocolate), (P Dazeley/mobile phone), 41 (M Lewis/Lena), 44 (C Windsor/Katya), 45 (M Douet/ cooking), 48 (D Madison/sons), 53 (J Lawrence/bridge), 55 (C Kunin/Keiko), 60–1 (R Van Der Hilst/Sydney aerial), 60 (D Jacobs/beach), 62 (B Torrez/Darren), 65 (M Clamer/ Calico), 76 (M Rogers/baseball), (D Madison/ice hockey), (M Lewis/swimming), 77 (J Polollio/Colin & Fran), (R Elliott/chalet), 81 (A Sacks/Archie), 84–85 (A Errington/man in Internet café), (J Franz/Internet address spiral), (M Westmorland/woman on beach with laptop), (HultonArchive/computer 1964), 88 (D Hanover/Enrique), 90 (W Scholz), 91 (S Grandadam/ river boat), 91 (C Kapolka/road), (B Handelman/orange train), 92 (T Main/fish), (J Kelly/chicken), 100 (F Wing/ Isabel), (K Mackintosh/Andy), (S Kobayashi/Mark), 101 (Kaluzny/Thatcher/wedding), (K Mackintosh/man on table-top), 107, 139 and 140 (H Kingsworth/Didier); GettyOne Telegraph pp10 (FPG/S Jones/hamburger), 14 and 138 (A No/Mayumi), (D Boissavy/woman from Oxford), 15 and 138 (S W Jones/Pierre), 19 (M Van Der Vord/Amy), 30 (G Bass/Rachel's family), 31 (VCL/father),

61 (VCL/windsurfer), (J T Turner/sailing), 76 (R Chapple/ walking), 80 (J Cummins/Sharon), (V Besnault/Lucy), (J Pumfrey/Ted), 82 (E Hesser/Tito), 92 (G Buss/salad), 49 (P Nicholson/photo of daughter in background); Oxford University Press staff p78 (L Evans/2 photos), (S Gray/2 photos), (J Fletcher/2 photos), (S Williams/3 photos); Courtesy of Philips p10 (television); PhotoDisc pp10 (photo in frame), 21 (Giovanni), 32 (tennis, swimming, skiing, ice-cream, beer, hamburger, coffee, oranges, spaghetti, wine), 33 (Bill), 37 (food), 39 (football), 76 (windsurfing, playing cards), 92 (tomato, fruit), 106 (Marco), 107, 139 and 140 (Rachel & Lara); Pictor International pp13 (Rick), 15 and 138 (Adam), 53 (Trinity College skyline), (Dublin doorway); Pictures Colour Library pp10 (house), 14 and 138 (Milan), 15 and 138 (Paris), 36 (5), 36 (4), 77 (D Henderson/beach), 92 (vegetables), 107 (Highlands of Scotland); Powerstock Zefa pp14 (Index Stock/Ted), 94 (Index Stock); Press Association p54 (M Fearn/girl in Internet café); Rex Features pp53 (bar), 66 (Presley); Robert Harding Picture Library pp27 (D Hunter/farm), 61 (A Hall/park), 91 (P Craven/blue train), (C Rennie/bus); Science Photo Library pp84–85 (D Parker/Hubble mission control), (Chauvet/Jerrican/researcher in field); Courtesy of Alison Snow p107 (New Zealand hot spring); South West News Service pp108–109; Still Moving Picture Company pp111 (D Corrance/view of Edinburgh, tourist office & museum), (K Paterson/tour bus); John Walmsley p90 (Alice); The Photolibrary Wales p27 (K de Witt/tractor)

With special thanks to:
St Clare's Oxford and their students for help with locations and models, and Swan School Oxford for their help with recordings

The Publisher would also like to thank the following for their help with providing a location:
Esporta Oxford, Eurocentre Cambridge, Caffe Uno Hertford, Copthorn Homes, Roberto Gerrards, Harlow College, Sky Penthouses, and Thomas Cook Harlow